W9-AUJ-582

*"Oh sing to the L*ORD *a new song,
for He has done marvelous things!"*

Psalm 98:1

a new song

Planted *by* Streams *of* Water
Psalms of Divine Wisdom

CONCORDIA PUBLISHING HOUSE • SAINT LOUIS

Copyright © 2008 Concordia Publishing House
3558 S. Jefferson Ave., St. Louis, MO 63118–3968
1-800-325-3040 • www.cph.org

All rights reserved. No part of this publication may be reproduced, stored in a retrieval system, or transmitted, in any form or by any means, electronic, mechanical, photocopying, recording, or otherwise, without the prior written permission of Concordia Publishing House.

Written by Jane L. Fryar, Rose E. Adle, Nicole E. Dreyer, Rachel C. Hoyer, Julie Stiegemeyer, Jane Wilke, Ruth Koch

Edited by Peggy Kuethe

Cover and interior illustrations ©shutterstock.com

Scripture quotations are from The Holy Bible, English Standard Version®. Copyright © 2001 by Crossway Bibles, a publishing ministry of Good News Publishers, Wheaton, Illinois. Used by permission. All rights reserved.

Quotations marked *LSB* are from *Lutheran Service Book*, © 2006 Concordia Publishing House. All rights reserved.

Quotation marked *LW* is from *Lutheran Worship*, © 1982 Concordia Publishing House. All rights reserved.

Quotation on p. 165 is taken from the *Concordia Self-Study Bible*: New International Version, copyright © 1986 Concordia Publishing House, p. 861. All rights reserved.

Definition in the Leader Guide notes for Monday, Week 1, Psalm 1, is taken from *Theological Dictionary of the New Testament, Abridged*, p. 548. G. Kittel, editor. Copyright © 1985 William B. Eerdmans Publishing Company, Grand Rapids, MI.

This publication may be available in braille, in large print, or on cassette tape for the visually impaired. Please allow 8 to 12 weeks for delivery. Write to Lutheran Blind Mission, 7550 Watson Rd., St. Louis, MO 63119-4409; call toll free 1-888-215-2455; or visit the Web site: www.blindmission.org.

1   2   3   4   5   6   7   8   9   10   17   16   15   14   13   12   11   10   09   08

a new song

Planted *by* Streams *of* Water

Psalms of Divine Wisdom

Meet the Authors

Jane L. Fryar enjoys serving God's people by writing and teaching. Her books include two titles focused on Servant Leadership, several LifeLight courses, the popular Today's Light devotional materials, and various other curriculums and resources for Christian teachers. Jane spends her spare time baking bread, lifting weights, and playing with Marty the Wonder Dog.

Rose E. Adle, proud member of the Concordia Deaconess Conference, lives in Fort Wayne, Indiana, with her favorite guy, husband Scott. She spent considerable time in Latin America as a tourist, a student, and an intern. In addition to this love for Spanish and salsa, Rosie also likes spending time with her wonderful family, playing tennis, games, and general fun. Oh yeah, and writing.

Nicole E. Dreyer says her childhood, her family, her teaching, and, yes, her cat are all a part of her children's devotions, curriculum, and books. But she explains that as she wrote these devotions for you, her peers, she happily drew from that well again, with some new perspectives and fresh insights that she prays will be as faith-enhancing for you in your devotional life as revisiting them has been for her.

Rachel Hoyer's family is her greatest source of joy—and of writing material. Rachel's daughter, Calista, is an aspiring writer and avid reader like her mother. Rachel's son, Sam, has a vivid imagination and shares his dad's sense of humor. Rachel's husband, Jeff, keeps the family's computers running so all this writing and creating is possible. Together, the Hoyers love to play games, make up songs, and relive their trip to Disney World.

Julie Stiegemeyer is a writer, a pastor's wife, a mom, and the caretaker of five pets in the flatlands of Indiana (two of the animals are aquatic frogs, so they don't really count since they hide under a rock most of the time). Every day is a new and interesting journey as Julie juggles family life, writing, part-time teaching, and volunteer work at church.

Jane Wilke is convinced that life is a journey of amazing twists and turns. Along the way, she has transitioned from being a teacher to an editor to a creative director to a specialist in communications. She loves traveling with her husband, is a frequent speaker, has a weekly inspirational radio spot, and looks forward to what God might have in mind around the next corner.

Ruth N. Koch appreciates the mystery of sitting before a blank computer screen and listening for the still, small voice of the Spirit—and then typing words on that screen. That those words may bless others is the gift and grace of God, that those words first bless her is the bonus! Mother of two daughters, grandmother of three girls, mental health educator and counselor—life is full of blessings and mysteries.

He is like a tree

planted by streams of water

that yields its fruit in its season,

and its leaf does not wither.

In all that he does, he prospers.

Psalm 1:3

Contents

How to Use This Book

 A New Song: Planted by Streams of Water is designed to help you grow in faith in your Savior, Jesus Christ, and to see how God works in your life as His precious and redeemed daughter. It is not meant to consume large blocks of your time. Rather, this book will help you to weave God's Word into your day and encourage and uplift you in your personal and small-group Bible study.

 A New Song: Planted by Streams of Water provides you and your group with six weeks of faith narratives based on biblical psalms. Each faith narrative was written by a real woman facing real-life issues—just like you. Each of our authors found help, encouragement, and direction for her life from God's Word and now shares her true story with you in her own words. Following each faith narrative, you will find questions that will encourage your own personal reflection and help bring forth meaningful and fruitful conversation in the comfort and security of your small-group.

 To derive the greatest benefit from your study, read the psalm in its entirety at the beginning of the week, and review it from time to time. Allow the authors' reflections on God's work in their lives to inspire your own. Write your thoughts and responses in the margins if you wish. Space is provided on the side of each page under the ✐ symbol. Answer the daily questions as best fits your unique situation and the time available to you, but consider how your responses can further group discussion. The prayers offered at the end of each narrative will help you to focus on the weekly theme and emphasis as you respond to God for His gifts of grace. Use the prayers as they are written, or make them your own by changing and adding to them as they touch your heart.

 Our prayer is that this book will enrich you as you drink deeply of God's life-giving water—the Holy Spirit—in your study of His Holy Word.

—The Editor

Suggestions
for Small-Group Participants

1. Before you begin, spend some time in prayer, asking God to strengthen your faith through a study of His Word. The Scriptures were written so that we might believe in Jesus Christ and have life in His name (John 20:31).

2. Take some time before the meeting to look over the session, review the psalm, and answer the questions.

3. As a courtesy to others, arrive on time.

4. Be an active participant. The leader will guide the group's discussion, not give a lecture.

5. Avoid dominating the conversation by answering every question or by giving unnecessarily long answers. On the other hand, avoid the temptation to not share at all.

6. Treat anything shared in your group as confidential until you have asked for and received permission to share it outside of the group. Treat information about others outside of your group as confidential until you have asked for and received permission to share it with group members.

7. Some participants may be new to Bible study or new to the Christian faith. Help them feel welcome and comfortable.

8. Affirm other participants when you can. If someone offers what you perceive to be a "wrong" answer, ask the Holy Spirit to guide her to seek the correct answer from God's Word.

9. Keep in mind that the questions are discussion starters. Don't be afraid to ask additional questions that relate to the topic. Don't get the group off track.

10. If you are comfortable doing so, volunteer now and then to pray at the beginning or end of the session.

Jane L. Fryar

Introduction

 week or two ago, I lunched with friends at one of my favorite restaurants—an eatery modeled after a French country café. I arrived early. Other patrons and even the wait staff were nowhere in sight. So, I sat alone, enjoying the sunshine under a striped canvas canopy at one of the bistro tables just outside the front door.

I had forgotten the way October's paintbrush could take the commonplace and use it to create enchantment. A riot of color shouted God's glory from the flower beds, hanging pots, vases, jars, and stone crockery that frame the area. A fountain nearby gushed skyward, creating rainbows. Puffy clouds drifted across a pristine sky. Near my table, water trickled from a pipe set into a brick column and dribbled its way into a pool beneath. Delightful! No other word quite captures the experience.

There's just something about the sound of water:

* ❇ Ocean waves pounding against rocks on the beach
* ❇ Lake water lapping at the shore
* ❇ A spring gurgling to the surface from deep inside the earth
* ❇ Sheets of rain falling from the sky, accompanied by a cacophony of thunder and lightning
* ❇ A leaping fountain
* ❇ A singing brook

Just thinking about any of these relaxes me. You too? Probably so. There's just something about the sound of water.

With that in mind, imagine living near a stream—a stream that never floods, never dries up, a stream that always sings songs of God's wisdom, songs of our Savior's love. Could your heart find rest in such a place? Could your heart call such a place its home? I know my heart could.

Resting in the Divine Wisdom

The faith narratives and Bible studies in this book take an in-depth look at six "wisdom" psalms. The psalms are poems— hymns, really—that describe life lived beside such a stream. Writing from their own experiences and, in several cases, using as examples their own personal fears, foibles, and failures to trust in the Lord's infinite love and power, the psalmists describe the delight of walking in the light of divine wisdom. They invite us to consider their insights. They hope to help us avoid the perils into which they have stumbled.

The faith narratives that accompany each day's reading from the psalms display a similar kind of raw honesty as the authors reflect on challenges they themselves have faced and the joys and peace God has given as they have followed the paths of divine wisdom revealed in His Word.

But what is this "divine wisdom"?

Well, certainly not the blather dished out in the off-the-top-of-my-head blog just this minute posted to the Internet. Certainly not the self-help advice offered by celebrity hosts on the 24/7 news channel, purporting to initiate us into the mysteries of making a great impression our first day on the job, or becoming a successful day trader on the New York Stock Exchange, or conditioning without injuries for our first marathon, or communicating our concerns to the family doctor who never seems to listen to us.

No, "healthy" and "wealthy" in that sense belong in a category quite separate from "wise"—at least insofar as Scripture teaches us to know true wisdom. Rather, the wisdom we will consider over the next six weeks bubbles up from a much deeper, much clearer, much more refreshing aquifer. This is the wisdom of heaven. It flows from the very throne of God. It sweeps us off our feet in wonder and amazement. It teaches us to live in peace beside the stream forever.

Psalm 1:3 describes the person who resides there:

> *He is like a tree*
> *planted by streams of water*
> *that yields its fruit in its season,*
> *and its leaf does not wither.*
> *In all that he does, he prospers.*

Sturdy roots. Abundant fruits. Those two phrases sum up our Lord's perfect will for us as we drink deeply from the stream of wisdom His Word provides.

Storms, Temptations, and Other Disruptions

Peaceful. Carefree. Unflappable. Do words like these capture what life is like when lived wisely beside the stream of God's

Sane

Word? Not always—as the faith narratives in this volume and the psalms you will study over the next six weeks will amply demonstrate. We might wish for something else, yet God's daughters receive no magical exemption from

* traffic tickets and loneliness;
* tears of shame and the guilt of self-righteousness;
* anger and envy;
* the pain of being the butt of unkind rumors and gossip;
* children who often refuse to listen and who sometimes disobey;
* doubt and financial worries;
* personal health challenges; or
* the pain that comes when loved ones die.

No, we are not exempt. In fact, the ironclad promises Jesus Himself has made to us include this guarantee: "In the world you will have tribulation" (John 16:33). As the old country preacher is alleged to have thundered, "When God sends you tribulation, He expects you to tribulate!" We may argue about the source of life's tribulations, but no one can seriously dispute the fact that life has plenty of them. No one can argue that even the heirs of heaven (that's us!) experience their share of suffering and frustration here on earth—and sometimes, more than our share.

Yet, even in the light of life's inevitable "tribulating," words like *peaceful, carefree*, and *unflappable* can and do capture what life is like when lived wisely beside the stream of God's Word. Just as surely as the psalms and the faith narratives you will read talk about trials and troubles, temptations and guilt, all of them also sound a crystal-clear note of triumph.

Despite our tribulations, at the end of the day, Jesus wins the day for His people on His cross and in His open tomb, washing away the guilt of our unbelief and misshapen lifestyles. The "tree" to which the psalmist points us in Psalm 1 may carry the weight of a hundred ice storms on its branches. Its top twigs may touch the ground as hurricane-force winds assault it. Its limbs may shatter and leaves drop off. But nothing, absolutely nothing, can uproot it. Our Lord Jesus has told us that storms will thunder and roar their way across our lives. But He has also promised to protect His people:

* [Jesus said,] "They will never perish, and no one will snatch them out of My hand." John 10:28
* "Blessed be the God and Father of our Lord Jesus Christ! According to His great mercy, He has caused us to be born again to a living hope through the resurrection of Jesus Christ from the dead, to an inheritance that is imperishable, undefiled, and unfading, kept in heaven for you, who by God's power are being guarded through faith for a salvation ready to be revealed in the last time." 1 Peter 1:3–5
* "We know that for those who love God all things work together for good, for those who are called according to His purpose." Romans 8:28

The Scriptures assure us that we are "those who are called, beloved in God the Father and kept for Jesus Christ" (Jude 1). Just think of it! Called! Beloved! Kept! Knowing and relying on that identity, the identity God granted to us in our Baptism, makes us truly wise, eternally wise. (There's just something about the sound of water—and the Word connected with it . . .)

Knowing and relying on the promises sealed to us in that water—promises renewed each time we kneel at the altar to receive Jesus Himself and all the gifts His life and death have won for us—works true peace for us and in us, and it generates in us an unflappable attitude, come what may.

Knowing and relying on the identity given to us through that water also activates in us an authentic witness that cannot be ignored or trivialized, even by those around us who claim no allegiance to our Savior. As our Lord Jesus told the Samaritan woman beside Jacob's well, the water He gives "will become in [us] a spring of water welling up to eternal life" (John 4:14). Water that overflows in such profusion can't *help* but spill into the lives of others.

Sane

Focus, Vocation, and Other Priorities

The wisdom psalms we investigate here ask hard but honest questions about life's seeming unfairness. The inspired writers do not answer all our questions. Instead, they continually point us back to our covenant-making, covenant-keeping Savior-God and the ultimate good He has promised to bring about for us, no matter how unjust or precarious our lives may seem at any given moment.

When this true wisdom—divine wisdom—resides in our hearts, we enjoy absolute security, the unshakable confidence that nothing—*nothing*—can hurt us.

This confidence, in turn, frees us for self-forgetfulness and service. No longer must we slave in misery for the false gods of gold and silver, wood and stone, to which the world system around us genuflects. Houses and land, wealth and power may come to us as blessings from the generous hand of our heavenly Father. Or they may not. Regardless, we do not cling to material possessions like some frightened kleptomaniac, vexed about missing out on the good life. Instead, we entrust ourselves into the hands of our heavenly Father, and we look to Him alone to supply the security, joy, and meaning He intends for us.

Then we roll up our sleeves and get to work, free to use all the blessings God grants—both material and spiritual—to serve our King Jesus by serving those around us who need our help. We

* change dirty diapers;
* organize this weekend's prayer vigil;
* create a five-year business plan for the company we have incorporated;
* cut the grass for an elderly neighbor;
* send our pastor a thank-you note;

No, in all these things we are more than conquerors through Him who loved us. For I am sure that neither death nor life, nor angels nor rulers, nor things present nor things to come, nor powers, nor height nor depth, nor anything else in all creation, will be able to separate us from the love of God in Christ Jesus our Lord.

Romans 8:37–39

Sane

* discipline our rebellious eight-year-old;
* listen with patience to a customer's complaint;
* volunteer to help at our daughter's volleyball tournament; and sometimes even
* relax in a tub of bubbles at the end of the day.

We do each of these and all of them for the glory of God (1 Corinthians 10:31), responding in wisdom to His various callings on our lives and relying on His forgiveness when we fail to fully communicate His grace to those whom we serve.

Our Savior-God has planted us beside the stream of His divine wisdom, and we take great delight in it. You see, there's just something about the sound of water . . .

Sane

Week One

Psalm 1

[1] Blessed is the man
who walks not in the counsel of the wicked,
nor stands in the way of sinners,
nor sits in the seat of scoffers;

[2] but his delight is in the law of the LORD,
and on His law he meditates day and night.

[3] He is like a tree planted by streams of water
that yields its fruit in its season,
and its leaf does not wither.
In all that he does, he prospers.

[4] The wicked are not so,
but are like chaff
that the wind drives away.

[5] Therefore the wicked will not stand in the judgment,
nor sinners in the congregation of the righteous;

[6] for the Lord knows the way of the righteous,
but the way of the wicked will perish.

Psalm 1:1

Blessed is the man who walks
not in the counsel of the wicked,
nor stands in the way of sinners,
nor sits in the seat of scoffers.

Inching In—The Path of Sin

 remember my first experience in a hot tub, and I have to be honest—I didn't like it much, at least not in the beginning. I tiptoed in gingerly with a grimace on my face. I wondered how anyone could claim to enjoy it. After I stepped in, I stood for a moment or two, trying to adapt my temperature to tolerate that of the searing water. My friends were all saying, "Come on, Rosie, just

get in. You'll feel a lot better once you do." Little beads of
sweat dotted my forehead, and I figured I'd be lucky if I
could spend two minutes in the steamy bubbles. Finally,
I managed to sit without feeling too uncomfortable. And,
much to my surprise, within a few moments, I was actually enjoying myself.

Perhaps you can't relate to this specific example, but
a hot tub isn't the only place that may call for some cau-
tious wading at first. It isn't unusual to see people edging
their way into something instead of diving in headfirst
and, before long, forgetting their original reluctance. A
little girl may sneak only one cookie from the jar at first,
fearful of being caught, but eventually she'll grab a bold
handful. A teenager might try a cigarette without any
intention of dabbling in anything stronger, but one thing
leads to another. A young woman might go a little too far
with her boyfriend, convincing herself she'd never get into
any real trouble, but with time, what once seemed risqué
suddenly becomes boring.

When I was eleven years old, I met a girl in the
neighborhood and started spending time with her. I knew
she wasn't the best influence. She used a lot of bad words,
and she sneaked out without telling her parents. I figured
it didn't matter, though, because I knew the difference between right and wrong. At first when she would do something bad, I'd look at her disapprovingly. But the more
time I spent with her, the more her disobedience seemed
kind of normal. As you can imagine, it didn't take long for
me to start picking up her attitudes and behaviors. My
parents sat me down and told me the importance of good
company, and they told me that little by little, I would
fall into the same bad habits as my friend. I couldn't deny
that they were right, although I didn't like to hear it.

Here in the first verse of the first psalm, we see
this concept played out. The psalmist starts by writing,
"Blessed is the man who walks not in the counsel of the

Rose

21

wicked." This seems a little extreme. Lighten up already! I mean, we can at least *walk* with wicked people, right? The psalmist goes on: "nor stands in the way of sinners." Well, okay; at this point, one might argue that standing right next to someone does imply a greater likelihood for behavior transference. And then comes the doozy: "nor sits in the seat of scoffers." By now, you're planted in the same seat, and then you really can't deny an association with the evildoer.

God speaks through this poetic progression to convict us with the realization of how easily we become accustomed to and comfortable with sinners and with sin itself. While the hot tub seemed extreme to me at first, before long, my once-sensitive skin

Instead of trailing after the wicked in your midst and instead of following your own sinful desires, remember who you are and whose you are—God's own child!

didn't even register that the water was scalding! This is true not only of *skin*, but also of *sin*. We have designations for sin to make ourselves think that some types are no big deal. Who hasn't heard of a "little white lie"? The concept of a gradation of sin makes sense. Certainly some sins carry more serious consequences for us and our neighbors. But don't be deceived: any and every sin is equally damning in God's court. His standard is perfection. "But as He who called you is holy, you also be holy in all your conduct, since it is written, 'You shall be holy, for I am holy'" (1 Peter 1:15–16).

Even the slightest infringement is enough to separate us from our Creator. The point is, we shouldn't dip even our little toe in the swamp of sin. Psalm 1:1 shows, through a logical sequence of exhortations, that we are to avoid even the first, seemingly innocent phase of moral deterioration. Any step (or stance or seat) that goes against God's Law is inexcusable! God knows, and human experience confirms, that even a mere rebellious thought is enough to bring grave consequences. The tiniest sin makes us unworthy in the eyes of our perfect Lord, and chances are that once we start, we will get ourselves in deeper and deeper, just like my experience in the hot tub and the case of my ill-advised friendship.

Rose

But if you're like me, you probably think you can keep your-self in check. God gives you the Law, written in His Word and on your heart, and you think you can inch right up to that line. You convince yourself that you can handle a little heat. In grade school, you thought it was fine to spend time with the mean girls because you knew *you* would never be like them. And this silly no-tion that you're above the sin of your company persists well into adulthood. You go for lunch with the office gossip, confident that *you* wouldn't engage in such mindless prattle. Or you smile and joke around with your attractive married neighbor, feeling sure that *you'd* never let it go further than light-hearted banter. The wicked have nothing on you . . . right? It'd be nice to think that way, but the company you choose actually matters; the world's in-fluence is strong. Hear the word of the Lord—the blessed person, the one who is righteous, will not sit with the wicked, or stand with them, or even stroll with them.

I not only *walk* in the counsel of the wicked, I *am* the wicked. And so are you. For we have all sinned and fallen short of God's glory (Romans 3:23). But take heart; all is not lost. If we are wick-ed, who, then, is blessed? Christ is blessed, for He alone resisted every sinful inclination. But it doesn't end there. Because of His righteousness, we, too, are made right with God. On account of His perfection, we share in His holiness. He felt a heat unlike any you or I ever have known—the sweltering blast of hades itself, which makes a hot tub seem downright frigid. And He did this to spare us from the fires of hell that we, in fact, deserve.

The Psalms were written for those who were within God's covenant, and this first psalm shows the chosen people how they were to live. So heed this word of wisdom. Repent and turn away from the sinful path you've laid for yourself. Don't inch in any farther. As the sharpness of the Law cuts you to the heart and you feel the deep guilt over the time you have spent stepping, stand-ing, and even sitting in the scum of sin, do not despair. When beads of sweat dot your forehead, make the sign of the cross, and cool your shamed, burning face with the life-giving, faith-offering waters of your Baptism. Instead of trailing after the wicked in

Rose

your midst and instead of following your own sinful desires, re-member who you are and whose you are—God's own child! His promises are everlasting. This is why the first word of the first psalm is a happy one. You are *blessed!* Together with His Word and Sacraments, your heavenly Father will strengthen you to walk in His truth and delight in His ways, as you return daily to your baptismal waters. So jump right in!

Prayer: Heavenly Father, holy and merciful Lord, You teach me in Your Word to avoid the ways of the wicked. Help me to live according to this wise coun-sel, that I might reflect Your love and mercy in all I say and do, and that others may see Your blessedness shining through me, through Jesus Christ. Amen.

Rose

monday

Personal Study Questions: Psalm 1:1

1. How do you understand the word *blessed* in verse 1?

2. With which illustration from today's faith narrative could you most closely identify? Why?

3. When has temptation caught your eye while you were walking? slowed you to standing? then convinced you to sit "in the seat of scoffers"?

4. All of us have fallen into sin. Jesus is the only "blessed" Man, the only blessed Person, who truly fits the description of Psalm 1:1. However, forgiven in Him and in His cross, you have inherited from Jesus the blessedness He earned for you! How will you use the blessedness God freely gives you in today's struggle with temptation?

Rose

Psalm 1:2

*But his delight is in the law
of the LORD, and on His law
he meditates day and night.*

For the Love
of the Law

I was twenty-one years old the first time I was pulled over for speeding; I was going 70 in a 55-mile-an-hour speed zone. I saw the flashing lights in my rearview mirror and my heart turned into a ball of mush. I was done for. As the officer approached my window, I was already apologizing profusely and saying how terrible I felt for the wrong I'd committed. Crestfallen and contrite, my face showed my guilt, and my hands were shaking. Upon hearing my blubbering admission of guilt and seeing the tears well in my eyes, the policeman surprised me by offering comfort instead

Rose

of chastisement. "Oh, don't worry, Miss. Don't feel bad," he said. "You probably didn't realize this, but there's a slight decline on this highway that may account for your higher speed. And there's also a pretty strong tail wind. There's no way you could have known that. It's all right." He wrote out a warning and asked me to please be careful, explaining that he wouldn't want me to get hurt.

I drove away very cautiously, breathing a deep sigh of relief and not believing the good outcome. I was spared a hefty fine; I felt like I had a second lease on life! Suddenly I loved the law and was quite happy to obey it! Well, maybe I didn't love the law itself; better put, I loved the man who had spared me from the wrath of the law. I even taped the warning to my dashboard as a reminder to watch my speed and drive responsibly. That slip of yellow paper was a visual reminder of the shame of being pulled over and the mercy of having my crime pardoned. And what do you know? My foot wasn't as heavy anymore! At least not for a while.

While no one likes to be caught, we all know that the law is a good thing. It exists for our protection, security, and well-being. Without it, scoundrels would run amok, and there'd be no accountability for crimes committed. Most of us who are (ordinarily) law-abiding citizens are thankful for the regulations established and enforced by civil authorities.

But God's Law just doesn't seem as appealing to us, does it? It seems to be more of a toilsome grind, perhaps because it is so much harder to keep. Civil law seems reasonable; God's seems anything but. Psalm 1:1 teaches us what we should not do. Psalm 1:2 teaches us the alternative. It's as though there are two ways offered to us. One option is the way of the wicked, but we know that this is not the blessed way. No, instead of fraternizing with the impious, we are called to delight in the Law of the Lord and meditate on it day and night.

How quick we are to hear a verse like this one and decide it is asking way too much of us. A clear pattern is already developing in this first psalm. We are exposed again as the sinners that we are. While we may fill our Amazon.com shopping carts with secular self-help books, we find little use for daily reflection on the Small Catechism, which actually reveals quite clearly the path to a blessed and fulfilled life based on God's Word. Jesus was the only one to steer clear of the wicked, and He was also the only one to exhibit and embody perfect obedience to God's will. As a young boy, He remained in the temple, studying the Law of the Lord. During His forty days in the wilderness, He quoted Scripture to combat Satan's tempting advances. And throughout the rest of His earthly life, He continued to honor His Father's will, even to the point of death on a cross.

The very fact that Christ's sacrifice was necessary proves that we do not keep God's commandments perfectly. And even when we try our hardest, we may find it difficult to see how the Law can be delightful. *Delightful?* Seriously? Would it not be enough just to obey God's Law? Do we also have to bask in it and relish it? What could possibly be delightful about two stone tablets that basically boil down to "Don't have any fun"? And meditate day *and* night? What's with the 24/7?

A definition of terms may be helpful here. This second verse of Psalm 1 isn't referring merely to the Law in the narrow sense—that is to say, God's rules and regulations. God's Law in the broad sense is more than just the Ten Commandments. They are certainly part of it, but not the sum and total. God's Law as it is used here in the Psalter means the Torah, what was then understood to be the entirety of God's instruction and teaching. The term *law* in Psalm 1:2 refers not merely to what we are to do but also to what God has done for us (the Good News, the Gospel). In other words, it encompasses all of God's revealed Word contained in Scripture.

Given the fact that the Law here relates not only to what we should do but also to what God did and does for us, there is a more attractive dimension to it. While we are sinful creatures, incapable of keeping God's commands, our big sin is met head-on by a bigger Savior, Christ Himself. *That* truly is a source of pleasure and joy . . . and, yes, a source of delight! When we meditate on it day and night—when we integrate God's Word into all of our

Rose

thoughts, words, and deeds—we understand that God's grace is not only a word of pardon but also a word of power. Christ living in us changes us!

As the police officer's grace inspired me to slow down and drive more responsibly, the far greater grace secured and procured by our Lord Jesus urges us and empowers us to change our wicked ways. Jesus said to the woman caught in adultery, "Neither do I condemn you," and then, in the same breath, "go, and from now on sin no more" (John 8:11). God's teachings, which once turned our heart into a ball of mush, now become the shape of our Christian life. We gladly hear and learn His Word, and we see that it is not just a mindless drudgery. We come to recognize the truth that His laws are established out of love and concern for our well-being. As a roadway speed limit sign is there to protect both us and the others on the road, God's mandates are designed to preserve us and our neighbor.

To this day, I remember the sense of relief I felt when I got off the hook on that speeding ticket. How much more should I experience a real and profound appreciation when reflecting on a far greater "get out of jail free" card that I have? When I stand before almighty God, I will have no excuse for my indiscretions. I may try to sugarcoat it: "Yes, I spoke ill of my boss, but I can't help it if she brings out the worst in me"; "Sure, I lost my temper with my friend, but she gave me cause!" Self-justifications such as these are useless. Sin is sin. God won't wink it away like the police officer did.

Yet, I am not condemned. I have an assurance that is faithful and true. And so do you. There is a piece of paper worth much more than a written warning taped to a dashboard. Your name is printed in the Book of Life. And you may have your very own written reminder to tape wherever you like—your baptismal certificate. Even if the original isn't accessible, write your Baptism birthday on a piece of paper and keep it in sight.

Although "the wages of sin is death" (Romans 6:23), you will taste only the Law's temporal wrath and not its eternal sting. You're spared, not because you have an excuse but because you

Rose

have a Redeemer who paid the price in full. So breathe a deep sigh of relief and drive on, with your eyes not in the rearview mirror but on the road ahead. Keep your heart and mind turned always to God's Holy Word, which you have been liberated to love. You're fine-free, and that's better than fine—that's delightful!

Prayer: Loving Lord, whose Word is truth, help me to see the infinite worth of Your teachings. Return me to my Baptism daily so I may be ever mindful of the pardon that is mine in place of the punishment I deserve. And lead me to live a new life as a law-abiding, law-delighting citizen of Your kingdom, through Your Holy Spirit and through Your one and only Son, Jesus Christ, who lives and reigns with You forever. **Amen.**

Rose

Personal Study Questions:
Psalm 1:2

1. Have you ever received a warning when you deserved a penalty? How do the feelings of the author of today's faith narrative reflect your own relief?

2. Rather than scoffing at God's Law, the blessed ones delight in it. Has the scoffing of others ever damaged your faith or caused you to call it into question? Explain.

3. The "law" in Psalm 1:2 refers to the totality of God's inspired Word, both Law (what God commands and forbids) and Gospel (the Good News of forgiveness and life through faith in Jesus and His cross). When do you take delight in God's Word?

4. How might you help yourself remember and reflect on God's Word more consistently ("day and night")? What difference would this make in your walk with your Lord?

Rose

Psalm 1:3

He is like a tree planted by streams of water that yields its fruit in its season, and its leaf does not wither. In all that he does, he prospers.

Teeming Streams and First-Rate Fruits

Rose

When I was twenty-five years old, I went to Caracas, Venezuela, to serve as a deaconess intern. I was bright-eyed and eager. Foreign missions had been my dream for a long time, so, for the most part, I was looking forward to it. Of course, I knew I would miss my family and friends dearly. And there was one other thing I expected to miss: the seasons. The way the Midwestern landscape reflects the passing of time has always enchant-

32

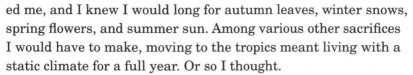

ed me, and I knew I would long for autumn leaves, winter snows, spring flowers, and summer sun. Among various other sacrifices I would have to make, moving to the tropics meant living with a static climate for a full year. Or so I thought.

When I arrived in Caracas, I learned that there are, in fact, seasons, just not the same ones I'd grown to know and love. There are definitely two distinct seasons in Venezuela: rainy season and mango season. They come in that order and are positively correlated. The more rain, the more mangos.

During rainy season, I never left my house without an umbrella. The skies were relentless. One time in the midst of a particularly rude downpour, I was racing up a hill when the streaming rainwater grabbed a sandal right off my foot and carried it away down the city street. During mango season, it was a different story. The sun beamed every day. Its happy rays matched the color of streets lined with mango guts. More than once, a sweet treat fell just inches from my head. And in my new sandals, I would slip and slide on mango pulp oozing from fallen fruits that had been crushed by cars or pedestrians. Dripping clouds one month brought dripping tree branches the next during the seasonal courtship in beautiful Venezuela.

For the first time, I saw the clear relationship between water and fruit. Without the water of the gray rainy season, there would be no green leaves and no yellow fruit. The country was a little dreary during the rains, but its fresh fruit economy sparkled later. And so it went. Rain poured down my face one month so mango juice could flow just as freely down my chin the next.

The third verse of Psalm 1 paints a striking picture of this water-fruit relationship. Verse 1 says what the blessed man is not to do, verse 2 what he is to do. And in verse 3, the Psalter's simile illustrates what that blessed person will resemble when his life reflects those salutary instructions: "He is like a tree planted by streams of water that yields its fruit in its season, and its leaf does not wither. In all that he does, he prospers."

How do you like that? Scripture says we will prosper in all that we do. That sure sounds good to me! Of course, as the

Rose

Scriptures teach and as human experience confirms, sinful beings like you and me consistently fall short of the picture of such arboreal health. Less like trees yielding succulent seasonal fruits nestled amidst crisp, fresh leaves, we are more like the useless vine, as Jerusalem was described in Ezekiel 15:1–8. Our sin, pervading every corner of our life, keeps our seasons chronically desolate.

When left to our own devices, we find no growth or hope in the midst of our rainy seasons of sin. That's because time after time, as we dawdle with the lawless and take no delight in the Law, our days are dark and dreary. We may drop a dollar in the Salvation Army bucket at Christmastime, but we do so in part because it makes us feel good about ourselves. Cooking a meal for a homebound neighbor springs more from compulsion than compassion. Altruism is all too often a fanciful philanthropic fiction in our lives. Although we try to do good works, the fruit still stinks. The depression that sinks in during long, dark winters takes root in our hearts, and our calendars seem stuck in the same old pattern of sin and despair.

Never forget that you have been planted—in fact, transplanted—through your Baptism. You were taken from the barren wilderness of wayward, parched rebellion and firmly planted by streams of living water—water with the Word, which works forgiveness of sins, life, and salvation.

Matthew 7:19 says that every tree that does not bear good fruit will be cut down and thrown into the fire. Well, if we're the trees and our sinfulness is the bad fruit, it doesn't take a genius to figure out what we're destined for. But wait! Remember that piece of paper you might have placed in plain sight yesterday? Look at it again. There's no expiration date on it. Its guarantee is fresh and timeless. Never forget that you have been planted—in fact, *trans*planted—through your Baptism. You were taken from the barren wilderness of wayward, parched rebellion and firmly planted by streams of living water— water with the Word, which works forgiveness of sins, life, and salvation. From the dead and dying stump of your own rotten soul, you were grafted to the vine that is Christ, the Word made flesh.

And Christ, of course, is living. His life is yours; so are His promises, which are not seasonal but ceaseless. He redeems not only you, but also your works. Your would-be good works were once pathetic and wilted and quite unpalatable. They were bruised on account of self-righteous motives and spoiled by the stain of sin. Now, though, they resemble the ripe, juicy fruits of the Venezuelan mango season. Our works—through the Spirit— are beautiful. They look like love, joy, peace, patience, kindness, goodness, faithfulness, gentleness, and self-control (Galatians 5:22–23). They look like love to one another (John 13:34). They look like the loyalty of Ruth. They look like the bravery of Jael. They look like the hospitality of Phoebe. They look like the humility of Mary, the mother of God.

But don't be overwhelmed by the examples of these faithful women. Remember that God uses humans—not super humans. Don't overglamorize what you're called to do. You will know that you are the good tree described in Psalm 1:3 when you simply do what God gives you to do through Christ. It is as basic as giving your sweaty son a glass of cold water when he comes in from a game of kickball. Or helping an older woman to the Communion rail on Sunday morning. Or feeding your neighbor's cat while she is on vacation.

There is nothing complicated about the process; it's as natural as rain and mangos. From Christ's mercy to you sprouts your mercy to others. As the water and fruit are inextricably bound together in the hills of Caracas, the hill of Calvary was no different. Christ, the very Tree of Life, hung from the tree of death. And on that hill, His outspread arms, the branches of His eternal love, produced good fruit—in fact, the *best* fruit. From His brow dripped sweat and blood. And from the pierced side of His crucified body flowed water and blood. The fruit of His labor on the cross is what we now taste at the Lord's Table when we receive His Holy Supper. And by this strengthening through the Sacrament, we are continuously grafted to our new life. This new life is filled with good fruit, born first from the waters of our Baptism and later preserved by the fertile food of Christ Himself, who fills our bodies and souls not just during certain seasons but

Rose

every day through His means of grace! The once-dark clouds of our souls are peeled back by the bright light of Christ's resurrection victory. There is no greater sweetness than the fruit of the tomb!

Prayer: Heavenly Father, Lord and Giver of life, You have promised me a new life that is firmly planted by streams of water. Guard and keep me in my baptismal faith so the fruit I bear through Your Spirit will be good for my neighbors and bring glory to You. Thank You for Your Son, Jesus, who bore the sweetest fruit of all that I may taste eternal life with You. It is in His precious name that I pray. Amen.

Rose

Personal Study Questions:
Psalm 1:3

1. The tree the psalmist describes is anchored, growing, and fruitful. How has God's Word and especially the Word made flesh, our Savior Jesus Himself, transformed you into a person of stability, growth, and fruitfulness, spiritually speaking?

2. Scripture never equates true prosperity with material wealth, earthly riches. But then, what *would* it mean for you to "prosper" in all that you do?

3. Today's faith narrative warns us against complicating or over-spiritualizing the process of bearing the fruit of faith. What examples does the author give of authentic fruit? When have you, "watered" and "fed" by God's Word and Sacraments, borne similar fruit?

Psalm 1:4–5

The wicked are not so, but are like chaff that the wind drives away. Therefore the wicked will not stand in the judgment, nor sinners in the congregation of the righteous.

"Clothesed" for Construction

My youngest cousin (at the time, a college senior) was sprawled across my bed, propped up on her elbows with a magazine draped over the pillow in front of her. We were chattering away while I picked out what I'd wear to work the next day. Casting a casual eye in my direction, she suddenly sat straight up and sputtered, "What is *that?*"

"What's *what*?" I asked, as she craned her neck and

Rose

38

squinted to get a better glimpse of whatever monstrosity she'd detected.

"That . . . " Her voice trailed off as her face crumpled into a look that combined disbelief with pity. "That . . . awful pink thing?"

"Oh, this?" I asked sheepishly, trying to hide a shirt that had no business being in my closet.

She laughed and told me with all the cousinly love she could muster that I should probably part with ol' pink. Knowing her fashion sense was far keener than mine, I quickly agreed. I even invited her to go through the rest of my closet and make recommendations. We spent the next hour and a half pulling out every article of clothing to my name. Even without her verbal assessment, I could tell by her reaction whether the garment would be restored to its hanger. Only those pants, skirts, shirts, and dresses that met the specifications of correct size and style were spared the wrath of her discerning eye. Anything faded, tattered, or outdated was cast into a bag marked "donate." Many items were banished from my closet forever.

This process of sorting and refining takes place regularly. We all dig through the recesses of our refrigerators to separate the must-be-pitched from the can-be-kept leftovers. Or maybe you've gone through files at work to find that more papers belong in the shredder than your desk. Whether it's a closet, fridge, or desk, over time, the bad mixes with the good, and eventually the two must be sorted.

In biblical times, threshing was the agricultural equivalent, but it was a far more violent process. The stalks of wheat were laid across the floor (a "threshing floor") and beaten fiercely. Then, the crushed pieces were launched into the air so the heavy grains—the good stuff—would fall and the light chaff—the bad stuff—would blow away in the wind. Without distinguishing the grain from the chaff, the use*ful* part of the wheat was use*less*.

While the third verse of Psalm 1 describes the healthy fruit and leaves of the righteous and prosperous, the next two verses give a dramatic comparison: "The wicked are not so, but are like chaff that the wind drives away. Therefore the wicked will not stand in the judgment, nor sinners in the congregation of the righteous." As there was no room in my closet for tattered clothing, there is no room for the wicked among the righteous. They have no business being there. They are driven away like the chaff beaten off of the good grains—banished forever from God's sight.

The imagery of this psalm calls to mind the New Testament parable of the wedding banquet found in Matthew 22:1–14. In this story, Jesus describes the kingdom of God as a wedding feast. At first, the king invites only the most distinguished guests, but they make excuses about why they will not attend. *Fine,* the king thinks, *they're no good anyway.*

All this, of course, pointed to the ultimate sacrifice—Christ Himself, who was laid out like wheat on a threshing floor and was beaten for our sakes. The chaff that flew off of Christ's crushed body—the very Bread of Life—was not His sin. It was ours.

Still wanting to provide a party for his dear child, he decides that if the elite are unwilling, and thereby unworthy, he'll find someone else to take their place! He tells his servants, "Go therefore to the main roads and invite to the wedding feast as many as you find" (v. 9). They go dutifully into the streets, announcing the feast with loud shouts and inviting all to attend. As you can imagine, unfortunate folks who never would have dreamed of feasting with the king rush to the banquet.

The king is delighted to have the wedding hall filled; after all, that was his plan! But wouldn't you know it? Someone doesn't belong. Some fool has showed up to the *king's* banquet in street clothes!

The king gives him the benefit of the doubt. "How'd you get in without wedding clothes?" he asks. But the poor pauper hasn't a prayer. He stands with his mouth open, speechless. The king's anger burns, and he summons his servants again, but this time with a different command: "Bind him hand and foot and cast him into the outer darkness. In that place there will be weeping and gnashing of teeth. For many are called, but few are chosen" (vv. 13–14).

In this parable, the king acts as a thresher and separates the good from the bad, the wheat from the chaff. The man in rags

Rose

is cast into the darkness; he has no business being in a banquet hall filled with finely dressed people. Who are we? Are we those who were allowed to remain in the hall or the one who was cast out?

You and I are daughters of Eve. We are her offspring, and as such, we have a great deal in common with her. We know God's will and we rebel against it. Then we feel the deep shame of our sin and want to cover it up, so we grab some leaves and string them together in an attempt to cover our embarrassment. We fumble about for any rag we can find to keep ourselves from being exposed as sinners. But God is not satisfied with this. God does not look at us in our fig leaves and think that our dress-up game is cute. Rather, He is like the king of the parable. Those who want to be in His kingdom, His utopian garden, must be in proper attire. But does He drive us away like chaff in the wind? Does He banish us from the congregation of the righteous? Of course not, for He is a merciful God, slow to anger and abounding in steadfast love.

How, then, are we clothed? A sacrifice must be made. God killed an animal in the Garden of Eden and clothed the mutinous couple with its skin. All this, of course, pointed to the ultimate sacrifice—Christ Himself, who was laid out like wheat on a threshing floor and was beaten for our sakes. The chaff that flew off of Christ's crushed body—the very Bread of Life—was not His sin. It was ours.

Through our Baptism into Christ, we were crucified with Him and raised in His new life. We entered the tomb of the baptismal font in grave clothes, for we were dead in our sins. In Baptism, our sinful nature was not patched up, but torn down. In those Word-ed waters we were reborn, re-created, and reconstructed. We emerged from the Church's womb in the white robe of Christ's own righteousness. Our tattered clothes were cast aside, and we put on the new life of the perfect tailor, our Savior, Christ the Lord.

Rose

Prayer: Mighty and merciful God, whose Son was beaten and crushed for me, forgive me for my ragged condition. Do not drive me away like chaff or cast me away from Your presence. But help me to live as one who has been clothed with Christ, a called and chosen daughter of the King, so that through Him, I might be worthy of the wedding feast You have prepared for me. In Jesus' name. **Amen.**

Rose

thursday

Personal Study Questions:
Psalm 1:4–5

1. Verses 4–5 contain only Law. The wicked are unstable and spiritually dead. No fruit springs from their lives. As you imagine such a life *here on earth*, what would be the worst part?

2. What does it mean to be a "daughter of Eve," as today's faith narrative puts it? In other words, what do you have in common with Eve?

3. The first audience to hear Jesus' parable about the king's banquet would have known that the guests coming to such a banquet received appropriate clothing freely as a gift from the king, the host. The person in street clothes evidently refused the beautiful, expensive robe he was offered.

   a. Why might someone do so?

   b. What "robe" has your King purchased for you?

   c. Why do some people refuse this robe?

4. We are all "wicked," "sinners," apart from a faith relationship with our Savior. We deserve to feel the full wrath of God in judgment, beginning now and continuing on into eternity. Instead, we will "stand in the congregation of the righteous." What words does 2 Corinthians 5:21 use to explain how this is possible? What would you like to say to Jesus in response to His incredible gift?

Psalm 1:6

For the LORD knows the way of the righteous,
but the way of the wicked will perish.

Two Ways and the Best GPS

Did you ever get lost in a store when you were little? Many of us have, and it's interesting to see how children react. Some keep walking aimlessly, totally unaware that they've been separated from their mom or dad. It seems as though they are oblivious to the fact that they don't have a ride home! Others realize what has happened and become afraid.

How about as an adult? Even as grown women, I doubt that any of us enjoy the sensation of feeling lost.

Rose

44

Are you an AAA member? Can't beat those unlimited maps! Or have you ever seen a commercial for a GPS (global positioning system) and thought, *A-ha! If I just have that installed in my car, I'll never get lost again!* We don't like to be lost because it makes us feel unsafe.

Anytime I travel to a new destination, I feel a twinge of anxiety. Will MapQuest guide me correctly? Will I make it there on time? Will I get lost along the way? Before I put the car in reverse, I study the directions carefully. Sometimes I even call others who have traveled the route before. I want to be confident before I set out.

Sadly, the truth is that no matter how many maps or navigational devices we use, they are not enough to help us reach our final destination. Because even if we're adept at directions and map reading, when we leave this earth, none of us can find our way to our eternal home on our own. We should feel like the child lost in a store who senses danger, recognizes her vulnerability, realizes her inability to protect herself . . . and is afraid. Our tears should be even more numerous than those of a lost toddler because our situation is much graver.

Right now, you may be wondering where I'm going with all of this. Follow me a little longer and you'll see where I'm heading. According to Isaiah 53:6a, "All we like sheep have gone astray; we have turned—every one—to his own way." Yes, like lost children in a store, we are wayward sheep, separated from our Good Shepherd. In this scenario, though, it is not simply an issue of physical separation, but also spiritual one. We are estranged in both body and soul.

This directional theme is precisely the focus of the final verse of Psalm 1: "For the LORD knows the way of the righteous, but the way of the wicked will perish." Scripture doesn't make it difficult to discern which is the better way, and there's no question as to what lies at the end of each path. The high road is, of course, the road to Zion. Any lane marked with the scuffled footprints of the wicked has a pretty obvious sign to alert us that it's the wrong way.

But the fact is, we're sinners. Even when we know the right

Rose

way, we choose the way of the wicked, time after time. We break the Commandments every single day. We do not love our neighbors as ourselves. And we do not love the Lord our God with all our heart, soul, and mind.

Studying the entirety of this first psalm makes it clear that we are not worthy to be counted among the righteous. We sit amongst the scoffers. We despise God's Holy Word instead of meditating on it day and night. We fail to yield the good fruit that we ought. We deserve to be driven away like chaff in the wind. And ultimately, these sins will be the death of us. "The way of the wicked will perish" because the holy God demands holiness from us.

On account of Christ's gift of forgiveness by grace through faith, we have the assurance that our death won't be the end either. We can be confident that we will never be lost, that we will always have a way home.

Like a little child lost in a store, we are defenseless. Nothing we say or do will make things right. We should not be oblivious to this fact; we should be scared. We should realize that we need someone bigger than ourselves, someone greater than ourselves to rescue us. The only one able to save us from our sins is the One without sin, who can pay the price to a holy, just God. And that person is God's own Son, Jesus Christ. He is the truth and the life, as it says in John 14:6, and ultimately, He is the way! He's not "a" way. He's not "one way among many." He is *the* way, the *only* way of the righteous. He died a perfect death on the cross so all of us who deserve the terrible fate of eternal and complete separation from God will instead be made right with Him.

It is on account of this reconciliation that Jesus was able to promise us in John 14:1–4: "Let not your hearts be troubled. Believe in God; believe also in Me. In My Father's house are many rooms. If it were not so, would I have told you that I go to prepare a place for you? And if I go and prepare a place for you, I will come again and will take you to Myself, that where I am you may be also. And you know the way to where I am going."

The "way" referred to here is the way of the righteous, the way of Christ Jesus Himself. Unlike an auto club membership

Rose

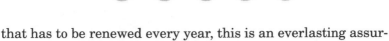

that has to be renewed every year, this is an everlasting assurance with an *eternal* lifetime warranty. The way of the righteous is sure because God has already walked the road. In Christ, He went before us. But don't be fooled. This does not mean the way of the righteous is a cakewalk. It does not mean we won't encounter gridlock or potholes or have to pass through rough neighborhoods. The righteous life doesn't mean the easy life. On the contrary, Scripture makes it clear that this life can be pretty awful, and, eventually, it will kill us. But Christ walked straight into death . . . and He walked back out. Something that looked like a literal dead end to everyone else didn't give God any trouble at all.

On account of Christ's gift of forgiveness by grace through faith, we have the assurance that our death won't be the end either. We can be confident that we will never be lost, that we will always have a way home. God's Positioning System—the best GPS around!—is revealed in the Gospel, and it is free! It started at the moment of Baptism and will guide and keep us in the true faith until life everlasting.

Prayer: Heavenly Father, whose Son is the only way to eternal life, lead me and guide me through Your Holy Word that I might walk in Your way. By Your Holy Spirit, drive me to repentance and contrition for my daily sins, and point me to the path of righteousness, that I might keep my eyes on Jesus and show others the way to Your eternal Kingdom. In His name I pray. *Amen.*

Rose

Friday

Personal Study Questions:
Psalm 1:6

1. Think about a time when you were lost, either as a child or as an adult. How would you describe that experience?

2. How does it comfort you to know that the Lord—your promise-making, promise-keeping Creator-Redeemer God—"knows the way of the righteous"?

3. Psalm 1 minces no words as it contrasts the paths and final destinations of those who receive God's gift of right-standing before Him by faith in Christ's cross and those who scoff and reject it. How does this clarity encourage you to pray for and witness to those who do not know and love Jesus as their Savior?

4. What comfort do you find in the words of verse 6?

Group Bible Study for Week 1
Psalm 1

1. Psalm 1 acts as a kind of gateway, an introduction, to the entire Book of Psalms.

   After exploring this psalm in some depth this week, why do you suppose the Holy Spirit led His people to place this psalm first in the Psalter?

2a. How do you define the term *blessed*?

   b. Are the righteous always "happy"? Explain.

   c. Why is "blessedness" better than "happiness"?

3. Psalm 1 contains several contrasts. Work together to list all you can find.

   a. In what way(s) do these contrasts warn us against sin and unbelief?

   b. In what way(s) do they encourage us to rely on our Savior, Jesus, and draw strength from Him for faith-filled living?

4. Someone has titled Psalm 1 "God Is Known in His Word" and Psalm 2 "God Is Known in His Son."

However, *both* psalms describe Jesus!

   a. Where do you see Jesus in Psalm 1?

   b. How is He the "tree" described in verse 3?

   c. How have you, too, become anchored, growing, and fruitful by faith in Him?

5. Think about your time in God's Word this week.

   a. How has it changed you?

   b. What new insights have you gained?

   c. What people, events, challenges, and opportunities do you see differently?

   d. What would you like to say to God about any or all of this?

Week Two

Psalm 34

¹ I will bless the LORD at all times;
  His praise shall continually be in my mouth.
² My soul makes its boast in the LORD;
  let the humble hear and be glad.
³ Oh, magnify the LORD with me,
  and let us exalt His name together!

⁴ I sought the LORD, and He answered me
  and delivered me from all my fears.
⁵ Those who look to Him are radiant,
  and their faces shall never be ashamed.
⁶ This poor man cried, and the LORD heard him
  and saved him out of all his troubles.
⁷ The angel of the LORD encamps
  around those who fear Him, and delivers them.

⁸ Oh, taste and see that the LORD is good!
  Blessed is the man who takes refuge in Him!
⁹ Oh, fear the LORD, you His saints,
  for those who fear Him have no lack!
¹⁰ The young lions suffer want and hunger;
  but those who seek the LORD lack no good thing.

¹¹ Come, O children, listen to me;
  I will teach you the fear of the LORD.
¹² What man is there who desires life
  and loves many days, that he may see good?
¹³ Keep your tongue from evil
  and your lips from speaking deceit.
¹⁴ Turn away from evil and do good;
  seek peace and pursue it.

¹⁵ The eyes of the LORD are toward the righteous
  and His ears toward their cry.
¹⁶ The face of the LORD is against those who do evil,
  to cut off the memory of them from the earth.
¹⁷ When the righteous cry for help, the LORD hears
  and delivers them out of all their troubles.
¹⁸ The LORD is near to the brokenhearted
  and saves the crushed in spirit.

¹⁹ Many are the afflictions of the righteous,
  but the LORD delivers him out of them all.
²⁰ He keeps all his bones;
  not one of them is broken.
²¹ Affliction will slay the wicked,
  and those who hate the righteous will be condemned.
²² The LORD redeems the life of His servants;
  none of those who take refuge in Him will be condemned.

Nicole E. Dreyer

Psalm 34:1–7

*I sought the L*ORD*, and He answered me and delivered me from all my fears.
Those who look to Him are radiant, and their faces shall never be ashamed. This
poor man cried, and the L*ORD *heard him and saved him out of all his troubles.
The angel of the L*ORD *encamps around those who fear Him, and delivers them.*

Never Be Ashamed

I don't know about you, but I am not very good when it comes to praying for myself. I have no problem praying for others—my family, my friends, even strangers. Whenever prayer requests come through my church's e-mail or from other sources, I stop for a moment and pray. But when I was in graduate school, and later, when I was job hunting, I don't remember praying for myself much at all.

I don't know why that is. Perhaps it's that "J-O-Y" Sunday School lesson stressed to me when I was a young girl. You know the one: "**J**esus and **O**thers and **Y**ou . . . put yourself last and spell J-O-Y!" Maybe I feel embarrassed to ask for what I want. Maybe I'm afraid of what the answer will be. Or maybe it's that I really don't know *how* to pray for myself.

Case in point: a few years ago, I bought my first house and began to make it a home. It wasn't as easy as I thought it would be. Although I was busy with teaching and church activities, I felt very alone in my own home. And so, for the first time, I found myself really praying for myself! I told God I was lonely and asked Him to bring someone into my life to fill the lonely place in my heart.

Like the psalmist, "I sought the Lord," and He *did* answer me. But the Lord delivered me, as He always does, in the way that was most pleasing to Him. You see, what I was praying for . . . well, what I *thought* I was praying for, was a man—someone to love and to cherish me; someone with whom I could build a life. God, in His infinite wisdom, knew best what was best for me. And so God did not send me a man.

He sent me a cat!

I've never been a cat person. I'm not wild about hair that's not my own covering my clothes and my furniture. But one October Saturday, not long after I had begun my prayers in earnest, a beautiful tortoiseshell calico showed up on my back deck. She was not the first cat that had been on my deck; I have several bird feeders, and strays had visited before. But there was something different about *this* cat.

I set out some milk; I could see the poor cat's ribs. She wouldn't come close, so I went back inside. The next morning, I was thankful to see that the milk was gone, and when I came home from church, she was waiting for me. This time when I went out and knelt down, she came over, put her head on my knee, and began to purr. I was hooked!

The rest of the afternoon, I thought about that cat until finally I decided I would "rescue" her. I went to the store for the

Nicole

bare necessities—litter box, litter, two bowls, a collar with a bell, some food, and a toy or two—and returned home to see if she was waiting for me again. At first, I didn't see her. It was getting dark and chilly outside, and I was worried. Then, suddenly, there she was, looking in at me!

My heart pounded as I gently slid open the door. Would she run or would she come? She didn't run. But she didn't come in immediately either. Instead, she cautiously put one paw and then another over the threshold until she was safely inside. Then she came right over to me, put her head against my leg, and purred. Right there on my kitchen floor, we became like a little family.

We never know what the answer will be when we pray, but we can be assured that God will answer, and He will always give us what we need, if not always what we want.

My cat's name is Bastet Grace—Bastet for a cat character in a series of books I enjoy, and Grace because it is by God's grace that we found each other. God, in His mercy, heard my cry and answered with what He knew I needed—something to love and to care for, *but also* something that needed the love and the care I could give, because Bastet Grace turned out to be a special-needs cat.

Our first few weeks together were a learning experience for me. Having never been a companion pet owner, I learned what food Bastet liked, what litter I preferred, and where she liked to hide. And we quickly got to know our new veterinarian well when Bastet developed a kitty version of the stomach flu and I learned to be a "parent" cleaning up after her illness.

Then the worst happened. While I was away for Thanksgiving, I received a call from the friend who was cat-sitting. Bastet was very ill! I contacted the emergency vet, who told me by phone that my cat had congestive heart failure and might not make it through the night. The vet also said she would understand if I didn't want to pay for the expensive treatment that might save Bastet since she was just a stray that I had only recently adopted. Just a stray? No way! I told her to do whatever was necessary to save my cat, and I headed back home.

The faces of those who approach the Lord in prayer "shall

never be ashamed" (v. 5) because God hears all prayers, even those for a beloved pet. And so, as I drove through the night across a cold, snowy, nearly deserted Pennsylvania Turnpike, my prayers for the next five hours were very specific: *Jesus, please get me there! Jesus, please save my cat!*

When I walked into the vet's at 11:30 that Thanksgiving night, they took me to the cages where Bastet was in a special oxygenated enclosure. There she was, huddled in a corner, looking small and sick and frightened. But when I touched the enclosure and called her name, she got up, came to the glass door, and rubbed her head against it where my hand was. The vet gasped. "Now I know why you came back!" she said.

The angel of the Lord *was* encamped around me as I hurried to get back to my cat in time, and he was encamped around Bastet in her special enclosure too. He was with my friends, who found Bastet in time, and he was with the doctors who saved her life. Today, Bastet Grace is a happy, healthy cat. She takes four pills twice a day, visits her own cardiologist once a year, receives more love than she had ever known before, and gives much love in return.

As for me, I have become a cat person after all. I have learned to tolerate cat hair, clean up hair balls, and "pill" a cat. I have learned much about cats specifically and animals in general, and I have become an advocate for them. But most important, I have experienced the power of prayer in my life in a way I never could have imagined. King David declared, "I will bless the LORD at all times; His praise shall continually be in my mouth" (v. 1). I may never meet the man of my dreams, but I praise and thank God for Bastet every day. Isaiah the prophet wrote, "Then you shall call, and the LORD will answer; you shall cry, and He will say, 'Here I am' " (Isaiah 58:9). Jesus Himself tells us to ask, seek, and knock (Luke 11:9). We never know what the answer will be when we pray, but we can be assured that God *will* answer, and He will always give us what we need, if not always what we want. I continue to pray for Bastet and for others, and I work hard on praying for myself as well. And when I'm in doubt, my prayer be-

Nicole

comes like that of the father of the boy with the unclean spirit in Mark 9:24, "I believe; help my unbelief!" and God replies, "Here I am."

Prayer: Dear Father in Heaven, help me to pray as I ought. Hear the cries of my heart, and in Your unfailing love, bless me with what You know I need, even if it is not what I desire. Help me never to be ashamed and always to boast in You, for You are my rock and my salvation. In Jesus' name. *Amen.*

monday

Personal Study Questions: Psalm 34:1–7

1. What similar personal experiences did the story about Bastet Grace bring to your mind? What thanksgivings did it spark in your heart?

2. The psalmist wrote Psalm 34 as an acrostic; each verse begins with the next consecutive letter in the Hebrew alphabet, as though recounting God's blessings "from *A* to *Z*." Think about your own blessings today. From *A* to *Z*, what would you name?

3. In this world, we encounter trouble, challenges, and heartache. Yet David encourages us to "bless the LORD at *all* times" (v. 1). When does praise come hardest for you? How might David's words in this psalm help you then?

4. The "angel of the LORD" (v. 7) might be a member of God's heavenly angel army or perhaps our Lord Jesus Himself. How can His protecting presence give you courage and hope "at all times" (v. 1) and especially today?

Nicole

Psalm 34:8–10

*Oh, taste and see that the LORD is good! Blessed
is the man who takes refuge in Him! Oh, fear the
LORD, you His saints, for those who fear Him have
no lack! The young lions suffer want and hunger; but
those who seek the LORD lack no good thing.*

Taste and See!

On the first day of school each year, my students and I fill out a "Me Sheet"—a questionnaire that not only helps me get to know my students better, but also helps them ease into their new class. The "Me Sheet" includes all types of questions—"What is your favorite color?" "Where did you go this summer?" "What do you love about your bedroom?" When everyone is finished, I collect the sheets, mix them up, and read portions of each survey aloud without sharing any names. The class then tries to guess whose "Me Sheet" I'm reading. They love guessing, and everyone has a great time. Before they

Nicole

know it, the first-day-of-school jitters are gone, and they've re-laxed. After I've read every student's sheet, I read my entire sheet as way for the class to get to know me better too. Then I file the "Me Sheets" away until the last day of school, when I return them so the students can see how much they've changed in a year.

It's also fun for me to see, from year to year, how I've changed. I've been filling out "Me Sheets" for more than twenty years now, and I have kept nearly all of them. Some of my an-swers change from year to year—the best book I read each sum-mer is different, as is the way I spend my vacation. What I watch on television, songs I listen to, and movies I enjoy change as well. Even what I like about my bedroom changes from time to time.

Many of my answers haven't changed over the years, how-ever. My all-time favorite movie is still *The Sound of Music,* my all-time favorite TV show is still *M*A*S*H*,* and I still love the music of The Beach Boys, no matter how old they are now! My favorite beverage has not changed either—iced tea. Whether it's unsweetened, or with a touch of lemon, or even very lightly sweet-ened, I just love iced tea! Hot tea, too, as a matter of fact, but *iced* tea is my favorite.

I can remember very clearly, as a young adult, the first time I realized I could have real iced tea all year long. As a child, we had iced tea in the summer. Later, when I was older, we some-times had "instant" iced tea the rest of the year, but not real brewed tea. No, that was only for summer. What joy it was for me when, living on my own, I began to brew iced tea in the winter. And imagine my euphoria when iced-tea makers came out on the market! I was in heaven! Now some of you may be saying, "Who can get that excited about iced tea?!" Well, to all of you, I ask, how do you feel about your gourmet coffee, your double latte, or your diet cola? *Taste and see!*

Journal writing is a daily activity in my classroom. One of the journal questions I always ask is "If you were stranded on a desert island, what food would you want with you and why?" I get answers from spaghetti to hot dogs to macaroni and cheese. I've even had a few students choose pig's feet! Every class always asks

59

if they can have more than one choice, and I usually allow two because I have two favorite foods as well—pizza and doughnuts! All of my students know how much I love pizza and doughnuts. In fact, it is both my love of tea *and* my love of doughnuts that led to Tea Time Fridays in my classroom.

Whenever we breathe deeply the scent of our favorite food, whenever we lick our lips and sigh with satisfaction, whenever we taste the goodness of the Lord, we are given a "foretaste of the feast to come" (LW, p. 169) and a powerful reminder of the most precious gifts coming from the Father of lights: life and salvation, through the suffering, death, and resurrection of the greatest gift of all—Jesus!

For Tea Time, each student has his or her own mug hanging on a rack in our classroom. On Friday mornings, I heat an extra pot of water and we fill our mugs with our choice of regular tea, flavored tea, or hot chocolate (with or without marshmallows) while the Tea Time student of the day passes out pastries, muffins, or doughnuts. Then we say grace and have our tea party. It is one of the highlights of our week, and no matter what has happened during that week— lost homework, detention, or disruption—no student ever loses the privilege of Tea Time Friday. *Taste and see!*

As you may have guessed, writing is an important activity in my classroom. Early in the year, as my students and I work together in writers' workshop, one of the first projects is a personal essay called "My Favorite Place." Each year, when I model that essay, I write about Rehoboth Beach, Delaware, where my family has vacationed since before I was born. I have so many wonderful memories of Rehoboth that I add to each year, but one of my oldest memories is also one of the most unusual. Why? Because it is triggered by a very powerful smell. It is not, as you might imagine, the smell of salt or surf or sand. Instead, the smell that always takes me back is the strong scent of creosote. Creosote? That oily liquid with a pungent odor that coats telephone poles? Yes, creosote, an antiseptic obtained from wood tar that is used as a preservative on telephone poles—and boardwalks!

Whenever I get a whiff of creosote, I am immediately taken

Nicole

back to one of my earliest memories—eating a Hershey bar on the boardwalk at Rehoboth. Back in the day, there were only a few after-dinner treats available to a child on the boardwalk—frozen custard (Dad always bought us vanilla), red candy apples (not until we lost our baby teeth), caramel corn (frequently), cotton candy (never!), and, as an extra special treat, a Hershey bar. Why was it such a special treat? Because the Hershey bar was dessert *after* dessert. We usually had an ice-cream cone every night, but every once in a while, Dad would buy us a Hershey bar too—ice cream *and* candy, on the same night! How decadent! And how delicious! *Taste and see!*

St. James wrote in his epistle that "Every good gift and every perfect gift is from above, coming down from the Father of lights" (James 1:17a). Iced tea, pizza, doughnuts, Hershey bars, and all the pleasures of food and drink that we enjoy are truly gifts of God, but they are more than that. Whenever we breathe deeply the scent of our favorite food, whenever we lick our lips and sigh with satisfaction, whenever we taste the goodness of the Lord, we are given a "foretaste of the feast to come" (*LW*, p. 169) and a powerful reminder of the most precious gifts coming from the Father of lights: life and salvation, through the suffering, death, and resurrection of the greatest gift of all—Jesus!

Jesus' precious body and blood, which we "taste and see" every time we partake of the Lord's Supper, were given and shed for us for the forgiveness of our sins. Whether our dessert cart is full or empty, our vacations exotic or modest, our thirst quenchers brewed or imitation, those who seek the Lord lack no good thing. We who fear Him have no lack because He has given His children what the "young lions" hunger and thirst for—green pastures and still waters, a full table of goodness and an overflowing cup of mercy, a foretaste of the feast to come that will follow us all the days of our lives until we dwell in the house of the Lord forever and share in that heavenly banquet together with all of the saints.

Give thanks to the Lord, for He is good, and His steadfast love endures forever. Give thanks to the Lord for *all* of His

Nicole

gifts—plain or fancy, regular or decaf, daily or rarely—for Jesus "satisfies the longing soul, and the hungry soul He fills with good things" (Psalm 107:9). *Taste and see!*

Prayer: Thank You, Lord, for all of Your good and perfect gifts—for food and drink and green pastures and still waters; for bread and wine and body and blood; for goodness and mercy and life and salvation; and for Jesus, in whose precious name we pray. **Amen.**

tuesday

Personal Study Questions:
Psalm 34:8–10

1. God's goodness toward us is so real we can taste it (v. 8)! When have you tasted His goodness and been blessed by it? Thank Him during your prayer time today.

2. When we "fear" the Lord, we come to Him in an attitude of reverence, awe, and respect. He works this "fear" in us through the gracious promises of His Word. What promises in Psalm 34 create godly fear in your heart?

3. What "good things" do you need today (v. 10)? Beginning with forgiveness of sins, ask your Lord to meet your needs for the sake of Jesus and His cross.

Nicole

Psalm 34:11–14

Come, O children, listen to me; I will teach you the fear of the LORD. What man is there who desires life and loves many days, that he may see good? Keep your tongue from evil and your lips from speaking deceit. Turn away from evil and do good; seek peace and pursue it.

The Voice

I'll share a secret with you: I committed a federal offense for which I've never served time! Admittedly, I was only about five years old. Here's how it happened. For the first twelve years of my life, we lived on a small cul-de-sac called Oak Court. And, yes, there were plenty of oak trees. In fact, during a summer thunderstorm one year, an oak tree fell into the middle of the court, narrowly missing the ice-cream man and his truck! But that's another story.

Our house on Oak Court was very nice. We had a large, fenced-in yard with a swing set and a log cabin

Nicole

64

playhouse, so there was plenty to do. Unfortunately, there were not many children to play with. There were only two others on my court—Jayne, who was two years older and already in school, and my best friend, Michelle, who was my age. But she went to afternoon kindergarten and I went in the mornings, so there was no one to play with until school let out.

One afternoon, I must have been bored, so I took myself a little walk around the court. When I got to the end, where our court met the much larger and well-traveled road, I turned around to come back. That's when I saw it—a beautiful envelope in someone's mailbox. I could hear that envelope calling, "Don't you want to see what's inside? Come here and take a look!" And that's exactly what I did. I marched right onto the porch, took the card from the mailbox, and opened it. It was a wonderful card, a birthday card. There was a little blonde girl on the cover, and inside was a little blonde paper doll that looked just like her. What really made that card so wonderful was a slit on the cover where you could insert the paper doll so it looked like the girl was holding it. I knew exactly how to do it, too, because I had received a card just like it for my birthday!

Right about then, I started feeling funny about opening that card, so I stuck it back in the ripped envelope, put it back in the mailbox, and went home. When I got there, my mom was on the phone. I knew from the look on her face that it wasn't good. It seems that the lady who lived in the house had seen me open the card and called my mom. Much to my five-year-old surprise, there's a law that says you're not supposed to open someone else's mail! Who knew? I'd never been taught that before. Still, somehow I *did* know. There was the little voice that told me I was wrong, that made me feel funny, and that made me put the card back. I didn't realize it at the time, but I had discovered my conscience!

Not long after that, Michelle moved away and there was only Jayne to play with. Jayne's house was four houses away, and to get to hers, I had to pass a much older house that was set back from the court, near the woods. It was a spooky old house, and

Nicole

we were afraid of it. We knew everyone who lived on our court except the people in that house. The only person we ever saw there was a tall lady with bright red hair who always dressed in black. Jayne, who was not only older but also more worldly, decided that the woman was a witch. According to Jayne, everyone knows you don't have to be nice to witches. Of course, I believed her—or I told myself that I did—so when Jayne came up with the "ring-the-doorbell-and-run" scheme, I joined in. Truth be told, I was scared to death, but I didn't want to be left out, so I rang the doorbell and ran.

The Father of Light promised that one day Eve's offspring would crush Satan's head, even as Satan tried to bruise the Offspring's heel. God's promise was fulfilled by the Word made flesh who is the Light that shines in the darkness, and the darkness, and the lies, cannot overcome it (John 1:5)!

Just then, Jayne's father, who was out mowing the lawn, saw me and said, "You'd better watch out, or the police will come and get you!" Now, I wasn't just scared. I was terrified! I ran home and hid inside my log cabin playhouse in the backyard. And later that night, according to my mother, I woke up crying when I heard a siren out on the main road. I was sure they were coming to get me. Even in my sleep, my conscience was at work!

"Come, O children, listen to me; I will teach you the fear of the Lord" (v. 11). How did I know what I was doing was wrong? While no one had specifically told me "Do not open other people's mail" or "Do not ring doorbells and run," I *had* been taught "Thou shalt not steal" and "Thou shalt not commit false witness against thy neighbor"; and while I might have been too young to understand the specific meanings of those commandments, I knew enough to understand that doing something that hurts someone else in any way is wrong.

The Book of Proverbs states "the fear of the LORD is the beginning of knowledge" (1:7a). Because my parents made sure I went to Sunday School and church and, when I was old enough, a Christian Day School, I learned to fear and to love the Lord at a very early age. With that love and fear came an inner knowledge of what was right and what was wrong, a conscience that reminded me to "turn away from evil and do good" and to "seek peace

Nicole

and pursue it" (Psalm 34:14). It was that little voice that had told me to put that card away and go home!

That same voice speaks to me today when it reminds me to "put the best construction on everything" and "if you can't say something nice, don't say anything at all!" But there are other voices, too, clamoring to be heard over my conscience. You know the ones I mean. There's the voice that says, "Go ahead, drive faster, or you'll be late for work, and then you'll really be in trouble." And the one that says, "She gave me too much change, but it's her fault. She should have counted it correctly." Another voice complains, "He got that promotion only because he plays golf with the boss." When that voice speaks, it's the same one Adam and Eve heard in the Garden, the one that called God's Word into question, the one that slyly asked, "Did God actually say . . . ?"

The father of lies will use any voice to get us to turn away from *the* Voice, the Spirit who whispers in our ear, "I am the LORD; I have called you in righteousness; I will take you by the hand and keep you" (Isaiah 42:6a). And, just like Adam and Eve, we, too, have the choice of which voice to follow—the lies or the Light.

I don't know about you, but more often than not, the father of lies has a field day with me. Try as I might, I often follow the wrong voice—I drive too fast, I swear, I complain about a co-worker. But each time I succumb to the lies, the Light calls me back and the "still, small voice" hears my cries from the depths of sin and despair and a guilty conscience. "If You, O LORD, should mark iniquities," wrote David, "O Lord, who could stand?" (Psalm 130:3). Thanks be to God that we know the answer, as David did: "But with You there is forgiveness, that You may be feared. . . . For with the LORD there is steadfast love, and with Him is plentiful redemption" (vv. 4, 7).

After Adam and Eve listened to the father of lies in the Garden, the Father of Light promised that one day, Eve's offspring would crush Satan's head, even as Satan tried to bruise the Offspring's heel. God's promise was fulfilled by the Word made flesh who is the Light that shines in the darkness, and the darkness, and the lies, cannot overcome it (John 1:5)!

Nicole

And if we walk in that Light, we will have fellowship with one another through the blood of Jesus—the Word, the Light, the Voice—that cleanses us from all sin (1 John 1:7–9). The God of peace *has* crushed Satan underneath your feet; therefore, "be wise as to what is good and innocent as to what is evil," for the grace of our Lord Jesus Christ is with you (Romans 16:19–20), whispering in your ear, "I have called you by name, you are Mine!" (Isaiah 43:1b).

Prayer: Father of Light, thank You for Your still, small voice that speaks to me every day through Your Word and through Your Spirit. When I go astray, forgive me for Jesus' sake, and call me always back into Your light. **Amen.**

wednesday

Personal Study Questions:
Psalm 34:11–14

1. In verses 11–14, David assumes the role of teacher. What recipe does he give for the good life?

2. What childhood memories illustrate for you the ways in which your Lord has shaped and sensitized your conscience? When are you thankful for your conscience?

3. None of us, of course, always likes to hear the messages our conscience sends us. We do not completely avoid gossip, slander, and lies. None of us turns completely away from evil or perpetually seeks peace. So our Lord Jesus did all this for us: He obeyed God's Law in our place. Now, God credits Christ's right standing in heaven's court as our own. What examples can you give of Jesus following the recipe you summarized in question 1?

4. What words of peace would your Savior speak to your conscience today? Find and read two or three favorite passages in your Bible, or discover a new favorite from John's Gospel, chapters 14–17.

Nicole

Psalm 34:15–18

The eyes of the LORD are toward the righteous and His ears toward their cry. The face of the LORD is against those who do evil, to cut off the memory of them from the earth. When the righteous cry for help, the LORD hears and delivers them out of all their troubles. The LORD is near to the brokenhearted and saves the crushed in spirit.

The Eyes and Ears of God

As Bastet's caregiver for the past few years, I have become fascinated with my cat's physiology. When she naps on the couch next to me, stalks across the floor after the gray cord from my hoodie, or sits for hours by the front screen door, watching the world go by, I am amazed by the complexity of this wonderful creature of our Creator.

One of my cat's more striking features is her green eyes. Set in her tortoiseshell calico face, Bastet's eyes really stand out. They are often the first feature others notice about her. Bastet's eye color is typical of most cats, whose eye colors run from green to yellow to gold to orange and combinations in between. Siamese cats and most white cats have blue eyes, although blue-eyed white cats are often deaf.

Not only do cats have colorful eyes, but they also see a colorful world, although not quite in the same way we do. At one time, cats were believed to be color-blind, but now we know that they predominantly see blue and green, as well as shades in that range, including some purples and yellows. Whether they recognize the color red is yet to be determined.

In my study of cats, I was surprised to learn that they have the largest eyes in relation to body size of any mammal. Cats see in three dimensions, as we do, but their protruding eyes give them a wider angle of vision than humans have; their field of view is close to 200 degrees, compared to a human's range of 180 degrees. Cats also have an elliptical pupil that opens and closes much faster than our human round ones, and it is protected by a third eyelid called a tapetum.

One of the habits I had to get used to with Bastet is her nocturnal prowling. Just as I am drifting off to sleep with my sweet cat seemingly sound asleep beside me, Bastet suddenly sits up, meows, walks right across me, and jumps off to wander the house in the middle of the night. Like her companion felines and larger wild-cat cousins, Bastet has incredible nocturnal vision and can detect brightness seven times better than you and I can. This is because a cat's retina has more rods (used for night vision and detail) than cones (used for daytime colors). Cats are also somewhat nearsighted—they see things best that are 6–20 feet away—so that in the dark of night, they are able to clearly identify closer objects, such as prey—or, in Bastet's case, my shoes in the middle of the floor. Ironically, the one place a cat cannot see, day or night, is directly under its nose, which is why Bastet uses her nose and not her eyes to find treats that are right there.

As amazing as cats' eyes are, created by God to serve such special purposes for their survival, they are not nearly as glorious

Nicole

71

as the eyes of the Creator Himself. David wrote, "The eyes of the Lord are toward the righteous" (v. 15). Our heavenly Father sees all that we are and all that we do, in the day and in the night, in the dark and in the light. And if that was all we knew about Him, we would be quaking in our boots because, as David goes on to say, the Lord turns His face away from "those who do evil" (v. 16). From those who do evil?! Uh-oh! If God really sees everything (and He does!), then He knows what I do, and He knows what you do, and it is not "all good." Who does evil? I do! And so do you!

When our feet slip, God's love supports us. When anxiety is great within us, God's consolation brings joy to our souls. The Lord is our fortress and the rock in whom we take refuge.

God sees the evil we do, but by His grace, He does not see us as evil. Instead, our loving Father sees us as righteous because He made Jesus, who had no sin, to be sin for us, so we might become the righteousness of God (2 Corinthians 5:21), and He has destined us for His glory since before time began! *Our* eyes have not yet seen, and our minds cannot yet conceive of all that God has prepared for those who love Him, who have been saved through faith by grace alone. However, like Paul, we fix our eyes not on what is seen but on what is unseen. For what is seen is temporary, but what is unseen is eternal (2 Corinthians 4:18b)! Therefore, we fix our eyes on Jesus, "the founder and perfecter of our faith" (Hebrews 12:2a), until that time when *every* eye will see Him. He will be our Shepherd and will lead us to springs of living water and will wipe away every tear from our eyes (Revelation 7:17).

"*. . . and His ears toward their cry*" (Psalm 34:15b). I love my cat's ears! They are so soft and so sensitive and so amazing. I love to watch her curled up in a ball at the end of the couch or next to my pillow. She appears to be completely asleep, but when I look more closely, I can see her ears twitch and even pivot at the slightest sound. That's because a cat's ears have 30 muscles (compared to our 6) that allow each of their outer ears to rotate independently up to 180 degrees and 10 times faster than a dog's. Bastet's hearing is also highly sensitive to sounds—five times

Nicole

more so than yours or mine, and even more finely tuned than a dog's acute hearing. Bastet can hear up to 100,000 cycles per second so that, with her incredibly sensitive pivoting ears, she can hear the smallest sound and pinpoint the exact direction and distance of its source.

David tells us that not only are the eyes of the Lord toward the righteous, but also that His ears are toward their cry. And Isaiah wrote that the arm of the Lord is not too short to save nor is His ear too dull to hear (Isaiah 59:1). Bastet's ears may pivot an incredible 180 degrees, but God's ears are omnipotently and omnisciently attuned, 360 degrees, to every cry of creation, from all creatures great and small. He hears our cries of pain and sorrow, our pleas for mercy, and even the silent despair of our hearts. "When the righteous cry for help, the LORD hears and delivers them out of all their troubles. The LORD is near to the brokenhearted and saves the crushed in spirit" (Psalm 34:17–18).

How does He do that? In Psalm 94, King David rhetorically asked, "He who planted the ear, does He not hear? He who formed the eye, does He not see?" (v. 9). The answer—for David, as it is for us— is "The LORD will not reject His people!" When our feet slip, God's love supports us. When anxiety is great within us, God's consolation brings joy to our souls. The Lord is our fortress and the rock in whom we take refuge. Through Jesus' suffering, death and resurrection, He has defeated for all time the power of sin, death, and the devil so we can boldly say, "Death is swallowed up in victory" (1 Corinthians 15:54b).

"The hearing ear and the seeing eye, the LORD has made them both" (Proverbs 20:12). Through the prophet Isaiah, our heavenly Father invites us to use our eyes and our ears to know His Son's victory. He calls to us and says, "Incline your ear, and come to Me; hear, that your soul may live. . . . *Seek* the LORD while He may be found; call upon Him while He is near" (Isaiah 55:3, 6). And Jesus Himself declares, "Truly, truly, I say to you, whoever *hears* My word and believes Him who sent Me has eternal life. He does not come into judgment, but has passed from death to life" (John 5:24). "Behold, I stand at the door and knock. If anyone

Nicole

hears My voice and opens the door, I will come in to him and eat with him, and he with Me" (Revelation 3:20).

Until that great and glorious Day of the Lord comes, "'Be strong; fear not! Behold, your God will come. . . . He will come and save you.' Then the *eyes* of the blind shall be opened, and the *ears* of the deaf unstopped. . . . [They shall] come to Zion with singing; everlasting joy shall be upon their heads; they shall obtain gladness and joy, and sorrow and sighing shall flee away" (Isaiah 35:4–5, 10).

Prayer: Hear, O people: the Lord our God, the Lord is One: O give thanks to the Lord, for He is good, and His mercy endures forever. **Amen.**

Nicole

Personal Study Questions:
Psalm 34:15–18

1. What insights did today's faith narrative add to your understanding of the Scripture reading?

2. Reread verses 15–16.

   a. What contrast do you notice in these verses?

   b. Who is "righteous"? Explain.

3. God's ears are "toward [your] cry" today! What will you whisper into your Father's open ear? What sense of boldness does the promise of verse 17 stir within your heart?

Nicole

Psalm 34:19–22

Many are the afflictions of the righteous, but the LORD delivers him out of them all. He keeps all his bones; not one of them is broken. Affliction will slay the wicked, and those who hate the righteous will be condemned. The LORD redeems the life of His servants; none of those who take refuge in Him will be condemned.

Rejoice, Rejoice, Believers!

What makes you cry? Anger, disbelief, or sorrow over an injustice? the unexpected loss of a loved one? Of course! But what else? Do you cry at significant family events or movies? a good book? a favorite song? or even, dare I suggest it, commercials? I do!

I get a little misty whenever there is a Baptism at church, but the day my nieces and nephew were all baptized together, this godmother was weeping! Other oc-

Nicole

casions at church warrant my tears as well. Maundy Thursday, when my confirmation class receives their first Holy Communion; on All Saints Sunday, when the tolling of our carillon bell coincides with the Commemoration of the Faithful Departed; the Easter sunrise service, while standing at the foot of a giant stone cross in a nearby cemetery.

Hymns can get to me too. "O Come, All Ye Faithful" and "Silent Night" on Christmas Eve and "Jesus Christ Is Risen Today" and "I Know That My Redeemer Lives" on Easter will elicit a happy tear or two. The hymn guaranteed to bring tears of joy, however, is "Holy, Holy, Holy," my all-time favorite.

Are there movies that make you cry? I love a happy ending, so just about any movie that ends "happily ever after" causes me to tear up. In fact, the very first movie that made me cry is still my favorite film. I was about five years old when my mother and grandmother took me downtown to see *The Sound of Music*. Even then, I loved everything about it—the songs, the children, the Austrian scenery, Julie Andrews and Christopher Plummer. And when the Von Trapp family went over those mountains on foot and the strains of "Climb Every Mountain" swelled, my little heart burst! Over the past forty years, I've seen that movie more times than I can count, and I still cry at the end.

Some TV shows also touch my heart. Seasonal cartoons are a sure cause for tears. No matter how many times I see it, when Linus recites the Christmas Gospel according to Luke; when the Grinch's heart grows three sizes; and when Kris Kringle marries Jessica beneath the Christmas trees on the holiest night of the year, I use a few tissues.

Those are tears of happiness, of course, but there are plenty of sad things that make me cry. Footage of the Twin Towers collapsing. Death and destruction caused by natural disasters, war, or criminal violence. Illness or injury experienced by others, especially loved ones. Migraine headaches!

And then there are tears that come at times that are both happy and sad: when my sister married and then moved out of state. When my students graduate and move on to middle school.

Nicole

77

When Jesus calls home someone I love. These are occasions when I shed tears of joy and of sorrow.

To someone who doesn't know Jesus, it would seem preposterous for me to say that when I cry at funerals, my tears are anything but tears of sorrow. But we know better, don't we? It's because of today's Scripture that we are able to cry *and* rejoice at a Christian funeral.

David tells us that despite our afflictions, the Lord will deliver us out of them all. And that is the sticking point for the nonbeliever, isn't it? My best friend, Lori, suffered with cancer. My grandmother lingered off life support for nearly ten days. My aunt never completely recovered from her stroke. The nonbeliever says, "Surely they were afflicted!" and we would agree that no one can make light of their suffering. But while those earthly afflictions were awful to bear, they could not and did not condemn the afflicted. As David declared, "The Lord redeems the life of His servants; none of those who take refuge in Him will be condemned" (v. 22). Lori, Mimi, Sa, all of my loved ones, and all of your loved ones who have taken refuge in Him have been delivered! There is no better reason than that to cry tears of joy!

And that is why we do cry mixed tears at our funerals—sad tears because we deeply miss the ones we love and joyful tears because we know that our loved ones, together with all the saints, are worshiping the Lamb before His throne and that one day we will be reunited with them.

If we take an even closer look at David's words, we will see not only what he declared but also what he prophesied: Jesus, who wept over the death of His friend Lazarus and who cried over Jerusalem, willingly went to the cross in our place. He who alone is righteous suffered the affliction of the wicked so we might be called "the righteous." And when the first part of David's prophecy was fulfilled, as recorded in John 19:36, Jesus was slain so we would not be condemned. And when He was buried and descended into hell, our Savior fulfilled the second part of David's prophecy: Jesus redeemed the lives of His servants, and He rose again on the third day so that all who take refuge in Him will never be condemned!

Nicole

And that is why we *do* cry mixed tears at our funerals—sad tears because we deeply miss the ones we love and joyful tears because we know that our loved ones, together with all the saints, are worshiping the Lamb before His throne and that one day we will be reunited with them. "For if we have been united with Him in a death like His, we shall certainly be united with Him in a resurrection like His" (Romans 6:5). How are we united with Him? "We were buried therefore with Him by baptism into death, in order that, just as Christ was raised from the dead by the glory of the Father, we too might walk in newness of life" (Romans 6:4).

So go ahead and cry at songs and at movies, at graduations and at weddings, and yes, at funerals too. Let your heart overflow with joy and with sorrow, but "let not your hearts be troubled," for Jesus says, "Believe in God; believe also in Me. In my Father's house are many rooms. If it were not so, would I have told you that I go to prepare a place for you? And if I go and prepare a place for you, I will come again and take you to Myself, that where I am you may be also" (John 14:1–3). And when Jesus brings us to be with Him, we will stand before the throne of God together with our loved ones and with all the company of heaven, and God will wipe away every tear from our eyes (Revelation 7:15–17)!

Rejoice, rejoice, believers! Alleluia! Amen!

Prayer: Heavenly Father, we praise and thank You for all of Your gifts of entertainment, of celebration, of life, and of death that make us laugh and make us cry. But chiefly, Lord, we thank You for the gift of Your Son, Jesus; for His suffering, death, and resurrection, so that we, together with the saints below and the saints above, are redeemed, delivered and righteous. In His holy name we pray. Amen.

Nicole

Friday

Personal Study Questions: Psalm 34:19–22

1. The author of today's faith narrative shares some of her own answers to the question "What makes you cry?" How would you answer this question?

2. Today, some teach that true believers have no problems, no tears. How does verse 19 answer that falsehood? It's bad news! But what promise, inspired by the Holy Spirit, quickly follows?

3. How does the life of our Savior illustrate the truth of verses 19–20? (Compare John 19:36.)

4. Verse 22 summarizes this entire psalm in a powerful, comforting way. What does it teach concerning God's heart toward you? What specific encouragement do you receive from these truths?

Group Bible Study for Week 2
Psalm 34

1. What new insights or particularly encouraging thoughts did the Holy Spirit bring to your mind and heart as you explored Psalm 34 this week?

2. The title, or superscription, on this psalm suggests a connection with 1 Samuel 21:10–15. The incident that sparked David's creativity in writing it evidently occurred before he became king, while he was still on the run from a murderous King Saul. Read about the incident in 1 Samuel 21:10–15. Then skim back through Psalm 34.

   a. Where do you see David's plight and rescue reflected in the hymn of praise he wrote?

   b. These are not the words of an "armchair quarterback"; the psalm was penned by someone who had narrowly escaped death at the hands of a very real enemy. How could David pray these words of praise and trust while still living in exile, while still facing danger and enduring considerable discomfort day by day? What truths can you take from this for your own life?

3. The "angel of the Lord" (v. 7) may refer to the heavenly hosts, God's angel army. However, some have also interpreted this phrase to describe our Lord Jesus before His incarnation.

   a. Read Genesis 32:1–2 and 2 Kings 6:17. For what purpose does the Lord's angel (or Angel) set up camp around God's children?

   b. What connection do you see between Psalm 34:7 and verses 8–10 that follow?

4. John 19:36 points back to Psalm 34:20. The prophecy of this verse was fulfilled in our Lord Jesus' earthly life. However, much more of this psalm also reflects Jesus' life, His suffering and death, and His resurrection victory.

   a. In what ways might we think of Psalm 34 as a song of triumph our Savior now sings?

   b. In which verses can you hear Jesus speaking directly from His heart and experiences to your heart and experiences? Explain.

5. Consider the phrase "the fear of the Lord" (vv. 9, 11).

   a. How does this "fear" compare and contrast with the "fears" of verse 4?

   b. What synonyms for godly fear can you find in the psalm itself?

   c. Would you say "the fear of the Lord" is essential to living the good life? Explain.

6. How does verse 22 summarize and fittingly conclude this psalm? In what way might it be an uplifting motto for the Christian life?

Week Three

Psalm 37

[1] Fret not yourself because of evildoers;
be not envious of wrongdoers!
[2] For they will soon fade like the grass
and wither like the green herb.

[3] Trust in the LORD, and do good;
dwell in the land and befriend
faith fulness.
[4] Delight yourself in the LORD,
and He will give you the desires of
your heart.

[5] Commit your way to the LORD;
trust in Him, and He will act.
[6] He will bring forth your righteousness as
the light,
and your justice as the noonday.

[7] Be still before the LORD and wait
patiently for Him;
fret not yourself over the one who prospers in his way,
over the man who carries out evil devices!

[8] Refrain from anger, and forsake wrath!
Fret not yourself; it tends only to evil.
[9] For the evildoers shall be cut off,
but those who wait for the LORD shall inherit the land.

[10] In just a little while, the wicked will be
no more;
though you look carefully at his place, he
will not be there.
[11] But the meek shall inherit the land
and delight themselves in abundant peace.

[12] The wicked plots against the righteous
and gnashes his teeth at him,
[13] but the Lord laughs at the wicked,
for He sees that his day is coming.

[14] The wicked draw the sword and bend
their bows
to bring down the poor and needy,
to slay those whose way is upright;
[15] their sword shall enter their own heart,
and their bows shall be broken.

[16] Better is the little that the righteous has
than the abundance of many wicked.
[17] For the arms of the wicked shall be
broken,
but the LORD upholds the righteous.

[18] The LORD knows the days of the
blameless,
and their heritage will remain forever;
[19] they are not put to shame in evil times;
in the days of famine they have abundance.

[20] But the wicked will perish;
the enemies of the LORD are like the glory
of the pastures;
they vanish—like smoke they vanish away.

²¹ The wicked borrows but does not pay back,
but the righteous is generous and gives;
²² for those blessed by the LORD shall inherit the land,
but those cursed by Him shall be cut off.

²³ The steps of a man are established by the LORD,
when he delights in His way;
²⁴ though he fall, he shall not be cast headlong,
for the LORD upholds his hand.

²⁵ I have been young, and now am old,
yet I have not seen the righteous forsaken
or his children begging for bread.
²⁶ He is ever lending generously,
 and his children become a blessing.

²⁷ Turn away from evil and do good;
so shall you dwell forever.
²⁸ For the LORD loves justice;
He will not forsake His saints.
They are preserved forever,
but the children of the wicked shall be cut off.
²⁹ The righteous shall inherit the land
and dwell upon it forever.

³⁰ The mouth of the righteous utters wisdom,
and his tongue speaks justice.
³¹ The law of his God is in his heart;
his steps do not slip.

³² The wicked watches for the righteous
and seeks to put him to death.

³³ The LORD will not abandon him to his power
or let him be condemned when he is brought to trial.

³⁴ Wait for the LORD and keep His way,
and He will exalt you to inherit the land;
you will look on when the wicked are cut off.

³⁵ I have seen a wicked, ruthless man,
spreading himself like a green laurel tree.
³⁶ But he passed away, and behold, he was no more;
though I sought him, he could not be found.

³⁷ Mark the blameless and behold the upright,
for there is a future for the man of peace.
³⁸ But transgressors shall be altogether destroyed;
the future of the wicked shall be cut off.

³⁹ The salvation of the righteous is from the LORD;
He is their stronghold in the time of trouble.
⁴⁰ The LORD helps them and delivers them;
He delivers them from the wicked and saves them,
because they take refuge in Him.

Psalm 37:1–11

Trust in the Lord, and do good; dwell in the land and befriend faithfulness. Delight yourself in the Lord, and He will give You the desires of your heart.

The Desires of My Heart

 remember reading Psalm 37:3–4 in sixth or seventh grade. I was flabbergasted at how cool God is. All I have to do is trust and all will be well. And if I trust enough, God will give me the desires of my heart. That's a pretty good deal. Talk about "When I was a child . . . I thought like a child" (1 Corinthians 13:11). A number of years later, I heard a pastor preach on these verses,

and I saw them in a whole new light. In my childlike thinking, what I hadn't understood about David's psalm was that last part: "He will *give* you the desires of your heart." I had focused on the end of the sentence: "the *desires* of your heart." I was twelve, so those desires probably included a date with Scott Baio from *Happy Days* and a new 10-speed bicycle.

But the crux of any sentence is the verb—the action. Here, the action is *give*. Let's deconstruct the sentence. Who is doing the giving? That's easy: God. To whom is the giving happening? Another easy one: me. (Yes, it actually says "you," but I'm taking this personally.) What is being given? Again, easy: the desires of my heart. Let's see. I desire a thinner body. I desire more sleep. I desire children who obey their mother all the time. I desire enough money in my bank account to pay the bills, to fix the deck, and to buy my husband the flat-screen high-definition TV he so desperately needs. There. That's a pretty good list to get God started.

Unfortunately—make that *fortunately*—for me, that's not what this passage is talking about. God isn't about to play Santa with my ongoing wish list. What He is prepared to give me is *desire*. When I trust in Him, when I delight in Him, when my focus is on Him, He will fill my heart with *desire* for Him, with *desire* for all that is good, not for worldly possessions or the body I had when I was twenty.

So what does it mean to "trust in the LORD"? What does it mean to "delight yourself in the LORD"? And how do I do those things when my wish list is growing and we're the only ones on the block who don't have a flat-screen high-def TV?

My husband and I learned about trusting in the Lord when we decided it was time to have a family. Mistake one: *we* decided. We didn't pray about it beforehand, we just decided. My husband and I are both the babies of our families. Once we make up our mind that something is going to happen, we tend to get our way. Our siblings will tell you as much. God, however, doesn't seem to go by this philosophy. Apparently, He thought it was high time we learn to operate on His schedule.

Rachel

We were having a hard time getting pregnant, and when we did, it ended in miscarriage—several times. We sought the advice of countless doctors. At the time, it seemed to me that everyone around us was having babies. I sat in the obstetrician's waiting room, surrounded by extremely pregnant women, wondering if I would ever experience their joy. A friend who had decided not to have children found herself accidentally pregnant. She and her husband were shocked at first, but then they were delighted. I told her I was delighted for them too. Another friend, who knew about our ongoing struggles, chose my birthday to tell me she was pregnant. I tried to be happy for her, but my heart was breaking. I went to more baby showers that year than I care to remember. Every time, I was the I'm-so-happy-for-you friend at the party. The first few times, I came home and melted in a puddle of tears. After I was cried out, I hosted a pity party and invited my good friend, Envy.

He taught me to "be still before the LORD and wait patiently for Him" (Psalm 37:7a). He taught my heart to delight in Him. He taught me that envy brings resentment and anger and frustration. Waiting and trusting in the Lord bring patience, joy, and unparalleled peace.

Envy and I did a lot of commiserating. Why weren't Jeff and I having a baby? We would be great parents! Why were all these other people having babies? They were probably going to be lousy parents! And what was with the news stories about teenagers having babies and dumping them in trash cans? The selfish ingrates! It just wasn't fair! Envy agreed.

If you'd asked me at the time if I was *envious* of any of these people, I would have explained eloquently that I knew I just needed to wait for the Lord's timing. It would all work out. But inside, I didn't want to wait for Him. He was moving too slowly. I didn't want to trust Him. He obviously didn't care about my feelings. Very deep in my heart, I knew I needed to wait for the Lord and to trust in Him, but closer to the surface, I was letting my friend Envy have a field day with my mind and my feelings. As the days went by, I let her have a greater hold on me. I wasn't listening to what God was trying to tell me.

"Commit your way to the LORD; trust in Him, and He will act. He will bring forth your righteousness as the light, and your

Rachel

justice as the noonday" (Psalm 37:5–6). The psalmist couldn't be much plainer. There's no gray area there. But as I wallowed in pity, with my friend Envy right beside me, I missed it all the same. "Commit your way to the LORD." Pray about it. Turn it over to Him. *Really* turn it over to Him. It took hitting rock bottom in our struggle and landing in the hospital, needing emergency surgery, for that command to get through to me. It was at that point that I was finally able to send Envy packing and let go of my resentment of all those other women. I relinquished control and told God I would listen for His voice. I would wait for His timing. I would trust Him.

And do you know what? He gave me the desires of my heart. He taught me to "be still before the LORD and wait patiently for Him" (Psalm 37:7a). He taught my heart to delight in Him. He taught me that envy brings resentment and anger and frustration. Waiting and trusting in the Lord bring patience, joy, and unparalleled peace.

In His time, and in His way, He also blessed me and my husband with two beautiful children. As I teach them to be patient, to wait, to trust, these lessons are reinforced in my own life.

As I studied Psalm 37, my eight-year-old daughter asked what I was doing. "I'm studying this psalm so I can write a devotion about it," I replied.

"Oh. Can I read it too?" she asked.

"Sure." I handed her the Bible. Verse 3 was at the top of the page. She read it aloud: "Trust in the LORD, and do good; dwell in the land and befriend faithfulness. Delight yourself in the LORD, and He will give you the desires of your heart."

She stopped reading. " 'Delight yourself in the LORD.' That's funny."

"What's funny about it?" I asked.

"Well, I'm picturing myself in my room with Jesus, laughing with Him and telling Him jokes. That's what they mean by 'delight in the LORD,' isn't it?"

Hugging her, I said, "Yes, dear, it certainly is."

What a wonderful God we serve! He took a path twisted with

Rachel

envy and resentment and straightened it. And on that path walks an eight-year-old, reminding her mother what it means to be delighted in a God whose love is so vast that He sent His only Son to die for us, so we can live—and laugh—with Him.

Prayer: Heavenly Father, thank You for being patient with me, even when I don't want to be patient with You. Thank You for taking my paths, made crooked with sin and envy, and making them straight. Mostly, Father, thank You for giving me the desires of my heart: to trust in You and to delight in You. In Jesus' name I pray. Amen.

Rachel

monday

Personal Study Questions:
Psalm 37:1–11

1. Like Psalm 34, Psalm 37 is an acrostic poem. Psalm 34 recalls God's rescue and blessings from *A* to *Z*. We might title Psalm 37 "The *A* to *Z* of Enduring Hardship."

   a. Skim Psalm 37. In what way does this title fit?

   b. Verse 1 introduces a central theme of the psalm. Summarize it in five to fifteen words.

2. What do verses 3–4 promise God will give His people? When has He done this for you in a way similar to that described in today's faith narrative?

3. The psalmist endures hardship and trouble while unbelievers all around him flourish.

   a. Why would this likely provoke the temptation to envy others?

   b. When have you faced this temptation for this same reason?

   c. Which words from verses 1–11 would help you the next time this occurs?

Rachel

Psalm 37:12–20

*The wicked plots against the righteous and gnashes
his teeth at him, but the Lord laughs at the
wicked, for He sees that his day is coming.*

He Who Laughs, Lasts

Do you ever feel like people are out to get you? I know. You're afraid to admit it because if you do, the armchair psychologists around you will label you paranoid. Forget about them for a minute and be honest with yourself. Doesn't it sometimes feel like the world is totally stacked against you and it's only the ungodly who prosper?

I admit that I sometimes feel that way. And when I do, I tend to get depressed and even angry. When I let

Rachel

that happen, my friend Envy returns. She fuels my anger and lets me seethe in it. And in my active imagination, I can do my fair share of evil plotting and gnashing of teeth. At those moments, I feel justified in my plotting because I'm not plotting against God's righteous (I'm counted in that number, after all); I'm plotting against the truly evil people of the world, those who would thwart me and my good intentions. Oops. I forgot. I'm supposed to be waiting for God, trusting Him, delighting in Him.

I want you to meet someone else who recently learned this lesson, my dear friend Sandy. At fifty, Sandy seems to be a magnet for misfortune. She and her husband, John, both struggle with their weight. John was self-employed, without disability insurance, when he started having severe health issues. He has survived colon cancer, but he continues to suffer from a number of other ailments. It is unlikely that John will ever be able to work again. Sandy supports them both on her teaching salary. She was recently diagnosed with diabetes and put on a strict diet to shed some of her excess weight.

One would think these health issues would be enough of a burden for wonderful people like Sandy and John to bear. But no. After John's battle with cancer, they decided to leave the house they'd lived in for almost twenty years and move somewhere that would be less work for John to maintain. The housing market was good, so they assumed their home would sell quickly, and their realtor echoed that sentiment. They had taken good care of the house. It was full of rich oak flooring, doors, and trim. It was in an established, quiet neighborhood. It had the makings of a quick sell. Eager for John to be able to take it easy, they purchased a newer, smaller home and moved in.

Months went by, and their old house didn't sell. Other friends were selling homes in a matter of days or weeks, but not John and Sandy. Theirs sat. They switched realtors. The new agent walked through the house and told them the wallpaper needed to go. It was too "country" and too "old lady." To prove her point, she slid her fingernail under a corner of wallpaper and ripped off a long piece. Then she announced that she'd be hosting

Rachel

an open house that Sunday, so they had five days to remove all the wallpaper and repaint.

Fast-forward seven months. The house was still on the market, and the realtor wasn't as quick to answer their calls. Finally, an offer. They settled on what seemed a fair deal. Then came inspection time. The buyers had a list of demands. They wanted a number of large-ticket items replaced even though they had passed inspection. With each demand, they threatened to walk away from the deal.

[The Lord] knows better than we do. He laughs, for He knows. Instead of focusing His attention on the wicked—because He knows they'll be their own destruction anyway—He dismisses their negative actions with His own positive ones. He cares for, protects, and upholds the righteous.

Every time I talked to Sandy in those weeks of negotiation, it seemed the buyers were making some new, outrageous demand. They wanted to move into the house three days prior to the closing, but not pay rent as is customary in such a situation. Then, already in the house, the buyers postponed closing yet again. Sandy and John were at the end of their rope—emotionally and financially. Sandy had been making two house payments for more than a year. They had borrowed money from relatives. They had mounting medical bills. And these buyers were ruthless and greedy beyond compare.

Sandy was feeling the pressure from all sides. Her teaching salary was stretched as thin as it could go. The few hours in the day she had left were devoted to a second, part-time job. She had to take John to appointments with various doctors—some as far as 175 miles away. And now these home buyers were doing everything they could to take advantage of sellers they knew to be behind the proverbial eight ball.

One day, in the middle of a debate with the buyer about a new roof, Sandy was near tears. "I'm a good person." Her voice cracked as she tried to hold herself together. "I've prayed from the beginning of this ordeal, asking God to help us find the right buyers so we could get on with it and so John could rest and recuperate. I haven't asked God why all this is happening—I know He has a plan. And I haven't asked Him to take away our health

Rachel

92

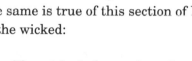

struggles. We know He'll bring us through that in His own way too. But I just can't take it anymore. I'm trying to do what He asks of me, but I'm surrounded by these buyers and their realtor and their inspector, who all seem to be pure evil."

Why am I sharing Sandy's plight with you? Is it to make you think, *Wow! Sandy and John have it rough. My life doesn't seem so bad by comparison?* Is it to gain your sympathy for Sandy and John? No. It's to help us all—you, me, Sandy, and John—put our burdens in perspective. Think about our lesson from yesterday, on the first part of Psalm 37. We focused on the *action* of the psalm. Our action is to trust in God, to wait patiently on Him, to delight in Him. God's action is to give.

The same is true of this section of Psalm 37. Look at the actions of the wicked:

* The wicked plot against the righteous and gnash their teeth at them (v. 12).
* The wicked draw the sword and bend the bow to bring down the poor and needy, to slay those whose ways are upright (v. 14).

Now let's take a close look at God's actions:

* The Lord laughs at the wicked, for He knows their day is coming (v. 13).
* The Lord upholds the righteous (v. 17b).

Were you expecting some smiting? Maybe a little fire and brimstone aimed at the wicked? Some good old Hollywood action? I know I was looking for a little retribution from the Almighty. But, as always, He knows better than we do. He laughs, for He knows. Instead of focusing His attention on the wicked—because He knows they'll be their own destruction anyway—He dismisses their negative actions with His own positive ones. He cares for, protects, and upholds the righteous.

Let's go back to John and Sandy for a moment. I don't want

Rachel

to leave them in limbo, in the middle of their distress. Sandy realized she wasn't doing herself any favors. She had let herself get consumed with worry about the swords and bows the wicked were pointing at her. So she read the rest of the story:

Better is the little that the righteous has than the abundance of many wicked. For the arms of the wicked shall be broken, but the Lord upholds the righteous. The Lord knows the days of the blameless, and their heritage will remain forever; they are not put to shame in evil times; in the days of famine they have abundance.

Psalm 37:16–19

Sandy changed her perspective on her circumstances. Ultimately, the house sold, and it's not her worry anymore. Her strict diet is helping. She has shed twenty pounds and is on the road to losing more. She feels better than she has in years. She and John can relax now that they have a budget for paying back their loans and paying off their medical bills. Did this happen overnight? No. But Sandy put her focus on God, and she decided to laugh instead of cry. Her laughter isn't malicious. It's a celebration of the plenty God provides in the moments of famine. It's a time of delighting in her risen Lord and Savior.

Prayer: Father, it's hard to laugh when the world is busy slinging arrows at me. I ask You to be my guide, to pick me up when I fall, to remind me that I am safe in the palm of Your hand. Thank You for Your positive actions in my life, Father—for laughing, for knowing, and for upholding me. In Jesus' name I pray. **Amen.**

Rachel

tuesday

Personal Study Questions:
Psalm 37:12–20

1. Today's reading from Psalm 37 provides a study in contrasts: the wicked and the righteous, material and spiritual abundance, earthly strength and divine protection, the temporary and the eternal.

   a. What similar point do all these contrasts make?

   b. How did these contrasts help the psalmist with temptations to envy the wicked?

   c. How did they help Sandy and John in today's faith narrative?

   d. How do they help you when you are tempted to envy the wicked and grow angry with them?

2. The psalmist seems to be saying, "Because the LORD is faithful, I can be faith-full." How does our Savior's faithfulness help you in times of hardship and stress?

Rachel

Psalm 37:21–26

*The wicked borrows but does not pay back, but the righteous
is generous and gives; for those blessed by the LORD shall
inherit the land, but those cursed by Him shall be cut off.*

Action Item:
Give Generously

When a major bridge collapsed in Minneapolis in early August 2007, all eyes were on the Twin Cities to see how they would deal with this tragedy. Many newscasters spoke of how "remarkable" the people of Minnesota were. Passersby climbed onto the collapsing bridge to rescue people from their cars. Brave souls jumped into the water of the muddy Mississippi River to help pull people from sinking cars. And all this before the

Rachel

trained emergency response teams arrived.

What compassion and bravery these people displayed! In a split second, they saw others in need and, without thought for their own safety, literally jumped in to help however they could.

The day after the tragedy, I saw an interview with an enterprising young college student who lived not far from the site of the collapsed bridge. It seems he was in his apartment with his roommate when they felt and heard a rumble. Looking out their window, they saw the bridge seconds after it collapsed. This young man quickly grabbed his video camera and headed toward the scene. His was the first "live footage" of the immediate aftermath of the collapse. The shaky images were played out hundreds of times by most of the major media outlets.

One reporter asked the young man what made him take his camera and if he'd given any thought to helping the people on the bridge. He said he knew there wasn't anything he could do to help.

What a stark contrast between the passersby who put themselves in danger because they saw other people in need of help.

We don't know who all those initial rescuers were. We celebrated their heroics only briefly. But we have watched this young man's video countless times, and his name is now recorded in the archives of many media outlets. It doesn't seem fair, does it?

I'm reminded of a friend who once told me that "fair" is a place where old men in overalls throw horseshoes for distance. That image makes me chuckle when the situations around me don't seem "fair" and when I'm tempted to whine about them like a four-year-old, or take a holier-than-thou view. As I look at Psalm 37, God doesn't say anything about doing what's fair, but He has plenty to say about how He expects us to live.

The wicked borrows but does not pay back, but the righteous
is generous and gives; for those blessed by the Lord shall
inherit the land, but those cursed by Him shall be cut off.
Psalm 37:21–22

Rachel

It's easy to think of that first line of verse 21 as being only about financial giving. I think I've even seen a version of it on a fortune cookie: wicked people borrow money and don't pay it back; righteous people give their money generously to others. It's also easy to dismiss generous giving as a duty required only of those who have a lot of money.

Let's think outside the box a little on that one, starting with our friends in Minnesota. Indeed, some people opened their wallets to help those in need after the bridge collapsed. There were also many stories of people opening their homes, giving of their time, preparing food, helping authorities determine who was missing. Counselors and pastors arrived on the scene to offer support and comfort to the injured and to the relatives of the missing. All of that counts as giving generously. So none of us can excuse ourselves from that part of the job description by saying we don't have enough money to give generously. It's not about money—it's about sharing with others what we have been given *freely:* our possessions, our time, our resources, our compassion, our aid, our abundant life in Christ.

How much easier does our job seem knowing that God walks beside us, catching us when we fall, and that He promises He will never forsake us?

So how is it that we learn to give generously? It is the grace and blessings of our heavenly Father that enable us to share our riches with others. What does it mean, then, to be rich? Ask my children. They'll tell you gladly. Reading is a big part of our lives, so our house is full of books. One day when she was six, my daughter announced, "We are rich with books." And so we are. Now we make it a point to share this blessing with others. Getting in the spirit of things, my son declared, "Cali and I are rich with toys." That was an excellent opportunity to ask if he thought we should keep that wealth to ourselves or share it with other kids who might not be rich with toys. Having just discussed sharing our book riches with others, it was easy for him to leap to "We should share our toys with other kids too!" Next it extended to clothing. Generous friends have passed along hand-me-downs from their children, so my children usually have more clothing than they need. Once,

Rachel

looking through a box of clothes for Sam that had just arrived from our friend Antonio, Sam asked, "Who do I get to make a box of clothes for?" I didn't quite follow him at first, so he explained, "Antonio gets to make a box of clothes to give to me when they're too little for him. Is there someone littler than me that I can make a box of clothes for?" He didn't know that I had been passing many of his outgrown clothes on to other little boys. I didn't realize he wanted in on the action. How silly of me to keep that opportunity to myself! Now Sam helps me box up his clothes for several younger boys. I was focused on saving time by doing it myself. It's wonderful to see how happy he is to share his clothes with others. Now, when I mention that something he's wearing is getting too small, he can hardly wait to wash it and put it in one of the special boxes to share with someone else.

Beyond sharing what we have with others, Psalm 37 also describes our walk with the Lord:

The steps of a man are established by the Lord, when he delights in His way; though he fall, he shall not be cast headlong, for the Lord upholds his hand. Psalm 37:23–24

We're not in this alone! When we do what God asks of us (our job description, as it were), He blesses us, helps us along the way, and holds us up when we stumble. Do you have a good picture of that? If not, feel free to use mine to help this concept stick in your head. When I was a kid, my siblings and I walked to school. On a particularly icy day (after a nice Nebraska blizzard), the sidewalks were precarious. I was six, walking merrily along my way, oblivious to the hazards beneath my feet. My brother was eleven, much more aware of how carefully we should tread. He walked beside me. In a split second, as I stepped on a sheet of ice, both of my feet went flying out from under me. In that same second, my brother grabbed me by the elbow and held me up until I could get my feet back under me. How much more does our heavenly Father watch our steps and hold us up when we stumble in our sin?

Rachel

Finally from the psalmist comes this exhortation that as we receive, so we should give:

I have been young, and now am old, yet I have not seen the righteous forsaken or his children begging for bread. He is ever lending generously, and his children become a blessing. Psalm 37:25–26

He makes it pretty clear that in his lifetime, he has never seen God forsake those who live as He has asked them to— waiting on Him, trusting in Him, delighting in Him, giving of themselves. Notice he doesn't say they are exempt from suffering. Remember all the swords and arrows in verses 14 and 15? But they are not forsaken by God, and that is good news indeed. How much easier does our job seem when we know that God walks beside us, catching us when we fall, and that He promises He will never forsake us?

Take a minute to write down the ways you are rich. Then write ways you can share that wealth with others. Wait on the Lord. Trust in Him. Delight in Him. He will give you grace and a desire to share your riches with others.

Prayer: Father, I rejoice in the abundant blessings You give me. I praise You for Your most precious gift of Your Son. Give me a generous heart to give of myself freely to those in need. In Jesus' name I pray. Amen.

Rachel

Personal Study Questions:
Psalm 37:21–26

1. In times of trouble and trial, we can easily find ourselves turning inward, worrying about our situation, and becoming self-focused. In contrast, the psalmist commends generosity and an outward "others" focus.

   a. When do you find generosity most difficult?

   b. Facing this temptation, of what does the psalmist remind himself?

   c. Might this work for you? Explain.

2. Our Lord provides for us! He even gave up His own Son into death to win our salvation. How could your Lord's mercy and provision instill a deeper sense of generosity in you today?

Rachel

Psalm 37:27–34

Turn away from evil and do good; so shall you dwell forever. For the LORD loves justice; He will not forsake His saints. They are preserved forever, but the children of the wicked shall be cut off.

The Letter of the Law

I noticed recently that I spend a lot of time focusing on the laws of the land—laws that govern my country, state, and city; rules and regulations that direct my children's school; policies that aid the operation of a church board; guidelines that serve those living in my house.

I even have several jobs that make it my business to focus on the rules. I'm in charge of the PTA newsletter at my children's school. It is primarily a venue for sharing information about the PTA's activities and projects around the school, but when the principal needs to remind parents (not children—parents) to follow the rules, she asks me to include an article about drop-off and pickup procedures or parking lot safety. I gladly oblige. After all, we need to whip some of these parents into shape. Who do they think they are, parking in the handicap-access spots because all the regular spots are full? I gladly climb on my principal-endorsed and principle-rich soap box and lay out the rules—in a "friendly reminder" tone, of course.

I also sit on a board at church. We are in the midst of revamping several of our programs for children and families. We are trying to be more structured so it's easier to train volunteers and to raise up lay leaders. Some of that means creating or revising policy and procedure manuals for these areas. With my organization skills and my writing and editing background, I'm a natural for this project. I love making sure everything is in order. And in a manual? All the better.

And at home, I'm the one in charge most of the time. When the kids were toddlers and preschoolers, there were days my husband would come home from work and I would tell him, "We instituted a new rule today. Here it is. . . ." We had agreed, after all, that my primary focus was taking care of the children and the house. Since I was home with them all day, sometimes new rules had to be made. And Daddy would gladly step in and support whatever was happening.

As I go about my rule enforcing, I like to think my mouth "utters wisdom" and my tongue "speaks what is just," as the psalmist says. But then I have a Bad Mommy Day—a day when I'm tired and cranky so I do and say things I swore I would never do and say—and I hear myself utter things like "because I said so" and "my house, my rules."

It's during those moments that I realize that once again, I have missed the point. I've been focusing on laws, rules, regulations, guidelines, and policies of man—some even of my own making. I've been living by the letter of the law, and doing my best to make sure others do the same. When I get in those tunnel-vision moments, I miss the spirit of God's Law.

Rachel

On Monday, we talked about delighting in the Lord—being still, waiting patiently for Him. In today's verses, we read that the righteous keep the Law of God in their hearts. So have we gone from waiting for His guidance and His timing and delighting in Him for all He has done to being rigid, rule-conscious vigilantes in just a few verses? Not at all. That's the tunnel vision I was talking about. I know I am guilty of getting so focused on the *letter* of the Law that I forget to *delight* in the Law. I know my children struggle with that too.

When my kids and I have a heart-to-heart about some rule they don't like, we talk about why we have rules in the first place. The five-year-old might tell me that rules are mean and he doesn't like them. He can't wait until he's the daddy and he gets to make his own rules. (These are the moments I'd like to record and play back for him in about thirty years.) The eight-year-old can extrapolate a little more, so she can usually come up with an explanation such as "You and Daddy make the rules to keep us safe. Like 'look both ways before you cross the street' is so we don't get hit by a car." Her brother can see her point on that one. He doesn't want to get hit by a car. But it's the finer points of rules like "Baseball can be played outside in the backyard, but not in the family room" that he's ready to debate.

By delighting in Him, focusing on Him, relying on His Word as our strength, we have freedom beyond compare. I don't know about you, but when I feel like I've been released from some burden that has held me down, I am nothing short of delighted.

His logic: "I want to play baseball. It's too hot outside. It's nice and cool in the family room. I'll be careful. Therefore, I can play baseball in the family room."

I can see his point. It *is* hot outside. I wouldn't want to play baseball out there, either. The family room *is* nice and cool. It would be a much more comfortable place to play baseball. He is a careful kid—very conscientious, generally not one of those bull-in-a-china-shop types. He would do his best not to break anything.

Ah, the sheer simplicity and beauty of a five-year-old's logic! But now I have to help him see, through his five-year-old eyes, why that won't work.

Rachel

Why is the rule there in the first place? Is it because I want you to be uncomfortable and play outside in the heat? No. Is it because the family room is all picked up and I don't want you messing it up? No, not really. (Okay, partly, but not really.) Is it because I don't think you'll be careful and try your best not to break anything? No. I know you'll be careful. I know it's not your intention to break things.

Sometimes we need to take ourselves out of situations that can harm us or harm things and people around us. Our goal is to make our home a safe place for everyone in it. If you're playing baseball in the family room and your sister walks through the room, the chance of her getting hit by a ball is pretty high. I'd rather she feel free to walk through the family room knowing there's no chance she's going to get hit by a baseball. We also need to take care of the things in our home. If a baseball hit Great-Grandma's antique anniversary clock up on the mantle, it would break. That would make me, Grandma, and Great Grandma very sad. If a baseball hit the fish tank, it might break. Then poor Franklin, Spot, Orange, and Dash would spill onto the carpet, and they might die. And we'd have one big mess to clean up.

Okay. Reality check. We wouldn't talk ad nauseam about all these things, but I include them here to make a point. It's important to know and understand the letter of the law. The more a person—especially a child—understands the basic reasoning behind a rule, the more likely he or she is to follow through on it. (Of course, we could spend a long time discussing age appropriateness and attention spans, but that's for a parenting book some other time.)

That understanding can lead to the more important part— what the psalmist is talking about—namely, delighting in the Law. "The law of his God is in his heart" (Psalm 37:31a).

What kinds of things do we hold in our hearts? Only those about which we care most deeply. Think about the things that mean the most to you. Don't they make you happy? Don't you *delight* in them? Then why not *delight* in God's Law, in His Word? Let's look for a moment at Psalm 1:2–3:

Rachel

105

But his delight is in the law of the LORD, and on His law
he meditates day and night. He is like a tree planted by
streams of water that yields its fruit in its season, and its
leaf does not wither. In all that he does, he prospers.

The Hebrew word for *law* here means so much more than a
list of "thou shalls" and "thou shalt nots." It includes the reason
behind the rules—God's will for our lives. His grace allows us to
move beyond the burden of the law. God's Law—His Word—isn't
just a list of rules. It's a safe haven, a stronghold, a source of
strength.

Remember getting the desires of our hearts from God? That's
the same God who gives us freedom through His laws. By delighting in Him, focusing on Him, relying on His Word as our strength,
we have freedom beyond compare. I don't know about you, but
when I feel like I've been released from some burden that has
held me down, I am nothing short of delighted.

That doesn't mean we're exempt from keeping the Law. On
the contrary, when we know and understand the "rules" God has
for us, and we realize that they are there for our safety, our protection, and our well-being, we can live freely within those boundaries. We keep His Law in our hearts, and it makes our hearts
sing praises to our amazing God.

Prayer: Heavenly Father, thank You for guiding
me every day through Your Word. Help me to live
each day delighting in You. In Jesus' name I pray.
Amen.

Rachel

Personal Study Questions:
Psalm 37:27–34

1. What logic, similar to that of the five-year-old would-be baseball player in today's faith narrative, do you sometimes create as you consider God's Law and your own sin?

2. In times of hardship, we can reject envy (vv. 1–11), recall God's faithfulness (vv. 12–20), and act with generosity and compassion toward others (vv. 21–26). In verses 27–34, the psalmist adds another strategy, pointing those who suffer to God's Word of comfort and promise. When has reading and contemplating the Word helped you through a time of hardship?

3. How could God's Word keep your foot from slipping (v. 31) into envy, anger, and unbelief?

Rachel

Psalm 37:35–40

The salvation of the righteous is from the Lord; He is their stronghold in the time of trouble. The Lord helps them and delivers them; He delivers them from the wicked and saves them, because they take refuge in Him.

Put Your Blinders On!

I once asked my friend, Liz, who owns several horses, why she put blinders on her daughter's horse before she let her ride. Liz explained that the blinders help the horse focus on the path ahead of him. She said since horses' eyes are on the sides of their heads, they are spooked very easily by sudden movements beside them. Liz said, "When this big guy is carrying my daughter, I want him focused on what's ahead of him, not distracted by what's around him. The blinders actually keep both rider and horse safe."

That made a lot of sense to me. Liz's words have

Rachel

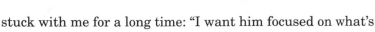

stuck with me for a long time: "I want him focused on what's ahead of him, not distracted by what's around him." Isn't that exactly what God wants for us?

When I first studied these last verses of Psalm 37, I was feeling overwhelmed by the wicked and ruthless around me, and I allowed myself to be distracted by them. It's hard not to be sometimes, especially when it all seems to be piling up around you.

A colleague told someone in a high-ranking position in our company that I'd made cutting comments to her to try to bring her down and undermine her success. I had done no such thing, but the company leader doesn't know me well, so she believed the other person. And she told a couple of other company leaders what she'd heard. My reputation was damaged, and I didn't even know it until weeks after the fact.

I created documentation to help company representatives share product information with customers. I e-mailed it to several colleagues for their feedback. One made a minor revision, claimed the document as her own, and sent it on to our home office. They loved the document and sent it out via global e-mail to the rest of the company reps, giving my colleague kudos for the idea.

I sat in a crowded hotel ballroom and watched as people who hadn't worked nearly as hard as I had and who had questionable ethics received recognition and rewards at our company's annual conference. They were lauded as leaders in the industry and held up as models for the rest of us to emulate. Boy, did they have the company owners snowed! And who were these sycophants clamoring around them?

Do you see where this is going? Did you get your engraved, embossed invitation to my pity party? Well, throw it away because that party's been cancelled.

The psalmist's words came at just the right time for me: "Mark the blameless and behold the upright, for there is a future for the man of peace" (Psalm 37:37). The "upright" include two of my friends, Andi and Brenda.

Andi works for the same direct-sales company I do. She has achieved moderate financial success and has earned several of the incentives and rewards the company offers. Andi's greatest success, however, is the way she presents herself to others. She is as close to blameless as they come. Andi has five children of her own, but she is "Mom" to many others—including some adults who thrive on her compassion and welcoming attitude. Andi is a wonderful Christian mother who lives to spend quality time with her family. She's the kind of person others are drawn to because she is so warm and caring. Andi operates her business with blinders on—staying focused on her faith and her family, and sharing a product she loves with others. The rest will come in God's timing, she says.

He is our stronghold. He is our "blinders," if you will. If we focus on Him and take refuge in Him, He will help us. He will deliver us. We don't need to worry about the wicked and the ruthless around us.

Brenda works for a different direct-sales company. She recently opened her home to a family of four who were about to become homeless. Brenda is a single mom with a special-needs teenager. She works full time at a residential facility for at-risk kids and runs her direct-sales business on the side. The last thing she needed to add to her life was caring for a family of four. But Brenda couldn't let them be homeless or just send them to a shelter, so she took them in. She is helping the mother find a job to get back on her feet. She enrolled the children in schools. She is encouraging them all to learn responsibility—they have chores around the house, just like Brenda's own daughter. Brenda took her family of two and made it a family of six without skipping a beat. She is another shining example of the upright.

When I focus on the things in my life that are unfair, on the undeserving wicked who have unwarranted financial success, on those who aim to ruin my reputation for their own personal gain, I can't help but get mired down in the muck and the mud. And then I can't go forward on the path the Lord has laid out for me or do much of anything productive. When I get in these ruts, I'm not a very good mom, I'm not a very caring wife, and I'm not a compassionate friend.

But I have been promised—and you have too—that "the salvation of the righteous is from the LORD; He is their stronghold in

Rachel

the time of trouble. The LORD helps them and delivers them; He delivers them from the wicked and saves them, because they take refuge in Him" (Psalm 37:39–40).

He is our stronghold. He is our "blinders," if you will. If we focus on Him and take refuge in Him, He will help us. He will deliver us. We don't need to worry about the wicked and the ruthless around us. They will eventually be destroyed.

I love what the apostle Paul told the Philippians; it's the same message the psalmist has:

But one thing I do: Forgetting what lies behind and straining forward to what lies ahead, I press on toward the goal for the prize of the upward call of God in Christ Jesus. Philippians 3:13b–14

My college forensics coach reminded us of Paul's words before every competition. He talked about our being citizens of heaven and that the day ahead of us was our opportunity to show others what a great place that will be to live. As we headed into competition, he said, "Remember who you are and Who you represent." That's a great reminder for a bunch of college kids and a way of life for us as adults. We are citizens of the kingdom. When we live our lives focused on the prize ahead, with our heavenly Father as our blinders, there's no room for the wicked and the ruthless to distract us. May God be your blinders today and always.

Prayer: Heavenly Father, some days I forget to put on my blinders. On those days, Lord, I get off the path. I get distracted. Please forgive me. Help me to keep my eyes on the prize, Lord, and to live my life as an example for others that they may see me as Your child. In Jesus' name I pray. Amen.

Rachel

Friday

Personal Study Questions:
Psalm 37:35–40

1. Compare the "tree" of verses 35–36 with that of Psalm 1:3. What accounts for the difference?

2. In what way(s) do the wicked succeed? How do they fail?

3. When are you most likely to forget to "wear your blinders," as today's faith narrative puts it? How is Jesus your "refuge" (v. 40) even then?

4. What makes verses 39–40 a good summary for this psalm?

Group Bible Study for Week 3
Psalm 37

1. Which faith narrative for the week did you find most helpful or meaningful? Explain.

2. As you compare the psalmist's experience with the hardships and turmoil you have faced, how realistic or true to life do you find it? Explain.

3. In what way is this a psalm about envy? patience? anger/frustration? faith/trust? joy?

4. The wicked set their own goals, devise their own definitions of success, and achieve what their hearts desire. Read verse 4 again. Some have read this verse to mean that our Lord will give us all the stuff, the temporary toys and worldly trinkets the wicked themselves crave. Suppose, though, the promise involves the Holy Spirit's work in our hearts to align our desires for ourselves with His own.

    a. Which of your heart's desires already, by God's grace, align with God's will for His children? How do you know?

    b. Which of your desires remain as yet unaligned? How do you know?

    c. What do you want to say to your Savior-God about your heart's desires and His promise in Psalm 37?

5. Someone has said, "When Jesus is all we have, we learn that Jesus is all we need."

    a. Would the psalmist agree? do you? Explain.

    b. How does verse 16 express this?

6. Tell about a time when adopting a generous, outward-focused stance helped you overcome stress or helped you work through a time of trouble. How did God's mercy toward you and His promise to provide for all your needs (Philippians 4:19) make it possible for you to act in this way despite your difficulties?

7. Complete this sentence: "The next time I am envious, worried, or angry, I will reread Psalm 37 because . . ."

Week Four

Psalm 49

¹ Hear this, all peoples!
  Give ear, all inhabitants of the world,
² both low and high,
  rich and poor together!
³ My mouth shall speak wisdom;
  the meditation of my heart shall be understanding.
⁴ I will incline my ear to a proverb;
  I will solve my riddle to the music of the lyre.

⁵ Why should I fear in times of trouble,
  when the iniquity of those who cheat me surrounds me,
⁶ those who trust in their wealth
  and boast of the abundance of their riches?
⁷ Truly no man can ransom another,
  or give to God the price of his life,
⁸ for the ransom of their life is costly
  and can never suffice,
⁹ that he should live on forever
  and never see the pit.

¹⁰ For he sees that even the wise die;
  the fool and the stupid alike must perish
  and leave their wealth to others.
¹¹ Their graves are their homes forever,
  their dwelling places to all generations,
  though they called lands by their own names.
¹² Man in his pomp will not remain;
  he is like the beasts that perish.

¹³ This is the path of those who have foolish confidence;
yet after them people approve of their boasts. *Selah*
¹⁴ Like sheep they are appointed for Sheol;
death shall be their shepherd,
and the upright shall rule over them in the morning.
Their form shall be consumed in Sheol, with no place to
dwell.
¹⁵ But God will ransom my soul from the power of Sheol,
for He will receive me. *Selah*

¹⁶ Be not afraid when a man becomes rich,
when the glory of his house increases
¹⁷ For when he dies he will carry nothing away;
his glory will not go down after him.
¹⁸ For though, while he lives, he counts himself blessed—
and though you get praise when you do well for yourself—
¹⁹ his soul will go to the generation of his fathers,
who will never again see light.
²⁰ Man in his pomp yet without understanding is like the
beasts that perish.

Julie Stiegemeyer

Psalm 49:1–4

Hear this, all peoples! Give ear, all inhabitants of the world, both low and high, rich and poor together! My mouth shall speak wisdom; the meditation of my heart shall be understanding. I will incline my ear to a proverb; I will solve my riddle to the music of the lyre.

Ears That Hear

eople who know me well know that, generally, I am not the most talkative person in the world. When I'm with my friends, I can be chatty, but much of the time, I am content to leave the talking to others. Knowing this, it would not seem that I would have a big problem with getting my twelve-year-old son to

listen to me; after all, it's not like I give him one long lecture after another. But just last week, I told my son to unpack his suitcase before going to bed. We had recently come home from a camping trip, and I didn't think it was unreasonable for my preteen to do his own unpacking. I was certain that I'd said the words aloud, but when I asked him what I had just asked him to do, he had no recollection. This, of course, was highly irritating and not simply a one-time occurrence.

So, I often find myself searching for new techniques or ways to get my son to listen to me. I have the mute-the-TV-while-I'm-talking method, the look-into-my-eyes-when-I'm-telling-you-something method, and the ever-popular put-down-that-video-controller-before-I-confiscate-it-forever-and-listen-to-me method. What especially irritates me is when my husband walks in the door from work, gives one simple instruction to our son in that special *dad* tone of voice, and *wham!* Not only does the boy hear his father, but he also obeys.

The first words of Psalm 49 are also about listening: "Hear this, all you peoples; listen, all who live in this world." This seems to me a sort of town-crier approach to getting people's attention, something similar to "Listen up!" or "May I have your attention, please," or, for the harder of hearing, "Open your ears and hear this!" This is a call to worship, a call for the people to listen to the Word of the Lord.

In order for people to listen, they must have ears that hear. In the Gospel accounts, Jesus is often quoted as saying, "He who has ears to hear, let him hear" (Matthew 11:15, for example). Obviously, Jesus' listeners had ears, but not all of those ears were listening. What was the difference? Why didn't they hear? Jesus is expressing the idea that *listening* and *hearing* are different. The sound waves may enter the child's ear, but does he know what was said? Does he act according to what he has heard? Was he really listening?

The truth is that all of us have stopped-up ears—or if we aren't completely deaf, we listen selectively. And we don't listen to the things we should listen to, but to things that actually hurt

Julie

us—and others. We hear the voice in our own head telling us that we *deserve* more stuff, stuff we don't really need—a better house, a better car, more possessions. The voice of temptation tells us to find that elusive happiness with a man who is not the one we married. Or that we would feel better about ourselves as moms if only we had children who were smarter, faster, or more attentive. We listen to the words of slander about a neighbor or the PTA president—and we not only listen to the slander, but we add to it. And we can't seem to get enough of it.

> *It is God's Word itself that opens my ears, God's Word that unstops them and quiets the distracting and confusing messages I hear all week. I realize, over and over, that Jesus, who truly does "all things well," also unstops my ears, pouring in the life-giving words of forgiveness and mercy.*

Think about it: when was the last time you told a friend something good about another person? When was the last time you gave someone the benefit of the doubt instead of rushing to judgment and gossip?

Television shows, movies, and even "chick lit" feed into this as well. The *Desperate Housewives* approach to life is backbiting, cat fighting, and adultery with the hunky gardener. But we can't blame society for the evils in our own hearts. The truth is that all of us have selective hearing. Our ears are full of the lies of the world, the devil, and our flesh, but we can barely stand to listen to a sermon that goes on for more than ten minutes. Do we have ears that hear?

Mark 7:32–37 describes an encounter between Jesus and a man who was deaf and had a speech impediment. The man was brought to Jesus for healing: "They begged Him to lay His hand on him" (v. 32b). What does Jesus decide to do with this man? Does He ignore the request? put it off until later? No. He listens, and right then and there, He puts His fingers in the man's ears and touches the man's tongue. Jesus looks to heaven and says, "Ephphatha!" which means, "be opened." And then the miraculous happens: with that simple act of touching the man's ears and tongue, Jesus unstops the ears and loosens the tongue. The formerly deaf and mute man is suddenly hearing and speaking plain-

Julie

ly. The disciples who witnessed the act "were astonished beyond measure, saying, 'He has done all things well. He even makes the deaf hear and the mute speak'" (v. 37).

Almost without fail, every Sunday, I sit during the sermon, listening to God's Word being expounded, and I find myself wishing I had gone to the midweek service or had been more diligent about my Bible reading during the week. My ears are opened again as, Sunday after Sunday, God's Word is poured into them in the liturgy, in the Bible readings, in the sermon. It is God's Word itself that opens my ears, God's Word that unstops them and quiets the distracting and confusing messages I hear all week. I realize, over and over, that Jesus, who truly does "all things well," also unstops my ears, pouring in the life-giving words of forgiveness and mercy.

At the scene of the transfiguration, the Father from heaven says of Jesus, "This is My beloved Son; listen to Him" (Mark 9:7). Our Jesus—who truly "does all things well"—also unstops our ears so we *can* listen to Him and hear the message that He has paid for our sins, removing them as far as the East is from the West. And it is Jesus who reassures us that He has given us all we need to support this body and life; that He cares for and comforts us through our families; that all of our needs are met and exceeded in Him, who truly does all things well. He gives us the open ears we need to hear the message of forgiveness, the absolution poured into our ears from the mouth of the pastor. The Lord Jesus opens our ears so we can hear God's Word, including the words of Psalm 49.

The theme of Psalm 49 focuses on the Christian's attitude toward money or "mammon." The verses of the psalm discuss such issues as being envious when others have more money than we do, coveting the riches of others, and how things in this world never last. All of this, however, will fall on deaf ears if we do not first acknowledge our sin and confess our Savior. Our Savior is Jesus, who has done all things well by dying on the cross to make the payment for our sins and who unstops our ears to hear the message of grace and forgiveness poured out to us through Word and Sacrament. And this message we gladly hear with wide-open ears.

Julie

Prayer: Dear Lord Jesus, thank You for unstopping my ears and for pouring into them the message of the forgiveness of sins. Thank You for doing "all things well," including providing all I need and promising me eternal life. Help me listen to Your Word with open ears and cling to it this day. In Your name I pray. **Amen.**

Sulie

monday

Personal Study Questions: Psalm 49:1–4

1. Psalm 49 is another of the Psalter's instructional or "wisdom psalms." What words in verses 1–4 might indicate this?

2. To whom does the psalm apply? For whom was it written?

3. What difference do you see between *listening* and truly *hearing*?

4. What keeps us from listening to the entire counsel of God and acting on it more consistently?

5. How does reflecting on Jesus' cross and open tomb help you when you find you have been neglecting God's Word?

Julie

Psalm 49:5

Why should I fear in times of trouble, when the iniquity of those who cheat me surrounds me . . . ?

For the Meat

The summer after graduating from college, my husband and I moved to Fort Wayne, Indiana, where he would begin studying for the pastoral ministry. While we both looked for jobs, we found low-rent housing, kept our expenses to a minimum, and utilized the seminary food bank. The food bank was—and still is—a wonderful place where we could get staples like flour, sugar, noodles, and cereal by spending points we earned through volunteer work.

Even with the help of the food bank, our budget was stretched very thin, and I found it very easy to slip into

Julie

122

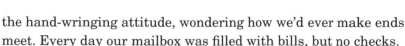

the hand-wringing attitude, wondering how we'd ever make ends meet. Every day our mailbox was filled with bills, but no checks. I lay awake at night, worrying about money. I tried to place my trust in Christ alone to provide, but when the bank account was nearly empty, it became a challenge.

One day, I went to the food bank to shop. I picked up a box of Hamburger Helper, thinking it might make a quick and easy meal between job interviews. When I opened the box to start dinner that evening, I was surprised to see folded dollar bills and a note fall out of the top flap and onto the floor. I reached down to pick up the folded papers. On the sticky note attached to the dollar bills was a message that read, "For the Meat." I sat down on the floor as tears flowed down my cheeks. Not only had some kind soul donated the Hamburger Helper, but he or she also had enclosed two dollars so we could buy the meat needed to complete our dinner. I felt like I'd won the lottery!

Two dollars and a note that read "For the Meat" would not seem like much to an outsider. But to me, it was a simple and thoughtful way that some Christian showed support of a seminary student and his family. It came at a time when I was frustrated that bills were abundant and paychecks were scarce. It came at a time when I began to doubt the loving, generous goodness of God and His provision for me. Hamburger Helper had never looked so good! And God had provided for me yet again through the generosity of His people.

Verse 5 in Psalm 49 begins, "Why should I fear in times of trouble . . . ?" This sounds very similar to other rhetorical questions asked by the psalmists. I immediately think of Psalm 27:1: "The LORD is my light and my salvation; whom shall I fear? The LORD is the stronghold of my life; of whom shall I be afraid?" In this psalm, the answer is given before the question is asked. The Lord is the answer to our fears. In Him, we need not fear.

In Psalm 49:5, it seems to me that the writer is asking and answering the question in the same breath. Why should I fear? Well, I shouldn't—the answer is *that* clear. But the reality is that I *do* become fearful when the future is uncertain. I *do* worry and

Julie

123

am anxious when my life is chaotic.

The truth is that I *do* fear in times of trouble. All of us do. We wonder, *What will become of us if I lose my job? What will we do if our children become chronically ill? Who will we turn to if the life we cling to falls apart? How will we make it to payday when the bills are piling up?*

It is precisely at these times when the grace of our Lord Jesus is sweeter than ever. Because, as Paul knew, we must realize that when we are weak, then we are strong. 2 Corinthians 12:10.

However, although we all worry, fret, and wring our hands over our problems, that does not make it right. Just because everyone does it doesn't mean it's not sinful. Who are we to question the providence of God? Who are we to whine and complain when God has given us all things for our good? And why is it that I never seem to learn the lesson that God indeed will provide all I need? The Hamburger Helper incident took place sixteen years ago, so why is it that I can't just get over myself and quit worrying? It's like I am asking and answering my own question in the same breath: *why should I be afraid? God will provide.* And yet, I need the reassurance the answer gives me over and over again.

It is precisely at these times when the grace of our Lord Jesus is sweeter than ever. Because, as Paul knew, we must realize that when we are weak, then we are strong (2 Corinthians 12:10). When we suffer, when we struggle in life, when we are the neediest, then our Lord's compassion becomes anew the precious jewel that we take for granted during the carefree days when we are eating a prime rib dinner instead of Hamburger Helper.

The term *incarnation* has at its center the root word *carne,* which is a Latin word meaning "meat" or "flesh." Think of the term *carnivorous,* which means "meat-eating." *Incarnation* is the word we use to describe how our Lord Jesus came to earth to save us. He became incarnate, that is, He became One who had flesh. Jesus, born of Mary, put on our flesh so He could die for the sins of the world.

This Gospel—or Good News—message about Christ is not meant to make us feel bad for Jesus or pity Him. He willingly,

Julie

voluntarily, lovingly became incarnate and died on the cross so He could give all good things to us. He takes our doubts, our weak faith, our worries about money, and substitutes His perfect work for us.

This is not a message to hear only once in a lifetime, however. What I've learned about myself, if nothing else, is that I need to constantly be reminded of the grace shown to me in Christ. Every day, in many ways, I fail my neighbor, doubt my Savior will care for me, give in to temptation, and wonder yet again how we'll make it to payday. And then I hope I'll remember to ask myself, *Why fear in times of trouble?* Because the answer is all too clear— I need not fear because the Lord Jesus who has graciously given me all things, including eternal life and all the riches of heaven, will certainly provide for me yet again. And He always does.

Prayer: Dear Lord Jesus, thank You for becoming incarnate in order to take on our flesh and die on the cross for our sins. Please help us to resist temptation, to help our neighbors, and to always trust that You will provide all we need for this body and life. In Your name we pray. **Amen.**

Julie

tuesday

Personal Study Questions: Psalm 49:5

1. In verse 4, the psalmist mentions a puzzle or riddle he hopes to solve. Verses 5–6 spell out that riddle in detail. Summarize it.

2. Everyone tends toward fear in times of trouble. That fact does not excuse our lack of trust in God, as the faith narrative indicates. Why do we still sometimes fall back on the excuse "Everybody's doing it"?

3. Instead of making excuses, we can make confession. How does Jesus' incarnation provide the comfort and encouragement that enable us to do so?

Psalm 49:5–9

[Why should I fear in times of trouble, when]
those who trust in their wealth and boast
of the abundance of their riches?

Clinging to Christ

In Mark 12:41–44, Jesus tells His disciples about a widow who gave a generous gift to the offering box in the temple. It was a small gift compared to the offerings of the rich, but Jesus says that it was all she had to live on, and thus her gift was praised more than any other. I wonder sometimes if this story reads almost like a fairy tale to modern hearers. When we think of fairy tales or *Aesop's Fables,* we remember homespun stories that teach some sort of moral lesson but that aren't intended to be literal prescriptives for behavior. We read the story of the widow's mite, perhaps, in a similar way. We may smile and nod at the widow's generosity, but do we really take it to heart? Are we willing—

127

like the widow—to give everything we have to live on?

Do you have a fire safe tucked away in a corner of your house or a safe deposit box rented at the bank? Many people do, including my family. Inside our safe deposit box, among the typical important documents, is some emergency cash. Having that little bit of emergency cash helps me sleep better at night. I know that if we get in a bind for some reason, we'll have a little spare money to tide us over. It's not much, but in case of a real emergency, it might be all we'd have to live on. But what if it wasn't a real emergency? Would I be willing to give all that we have away?

Psalm 49:5–6 reads, "Why should I fear in times of trouble, when the iniquity of those who cheat me surrounds me, those who trust in their wealth and boast of the abundance of their riches?" What does it mean to trust in wealth? Well, when I think about giving my very last penny—my emergency cash and all—to the church, my palms start to sweat, and I get a lump in the pit of my stomach. But isn't that feeling of nervousness, of not being able to let go, in itself, trusting in my money to save me?

The widow gave a little and it counted for much. The Savior gave all and it counted for everything; all of eternity is opened to us because of His gracious payment for sin. He gave all He could give—and He did it all for us.

The line in the story of the widow's mite that amazes me is that she gave "everything she had to live on." The widow is the antithesis of the one who trusts in wealth or riches as is described in Psalm 49. Even if the widow also had sweaty palms and a lump in the pit of her stomach when her two copper coins clinked in the offering box, her actions showed a different story. She didn't cling to this world. What the widow shows in her actions is that despite her need and the fact that she had no husband to provide for her, she knew she could count on God. She merely acknowledged this truth by giving her gifts to the temple—because all things really belong to God anyway.

This is similar to a king and his kingdom. The king owns the land, rules the land, and is its lawful guardian. As such, he can delegate portions of it to others to care for. A steward, then, takes charge of the land or property, but does not own it. I find this a

Julie

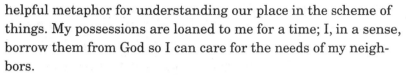

helpful metaphor for understanding our place in the scheme of things. My possessions are loaned to me for a time; I, in a sense, borrow them from God so I can care for the needs of my neighbors.

Moving to a new home can be a good lesson in how we should not trust in wealth or material possessions. When my family moved to a new state, it was a full twelve months of adjustments and changes. This experience taught me, once again, that things are only things, and what matters is my faith, my friendships, and my family. Of course, we brought our stuff with us, but our lives are very different here, our home is different. Moving can be one of those lifetime experiences that can teach you to know that nothing in this world endures. James 1:11 echoes the words of Psalm 49: "For the sun rises with its scorching heat and withers the grass; its flower falls, and its beauty perishes. So also will the rich man fade away in the midst of his pursuits." The transitory nature of life leads us to look for something enduring, something permanent.

Second, moving or any other major life event can help us cling to the One who never changes. My pastor-husband left a loving parish to work on a seminary campus. His work here has been challenging and enjoyable. But it was very difficult to leave behind those dear parishioners who were like a second family to us. Two things that eased my sense of loss during that time were stained glass windows of Jesus, our Good Shepherd.

In our church in Pittsburgh, Pennsylvania, the Good Shepherd window that looked over the choir loft always served as a powerful and comforting reminder to me of the loving compassion and care of my Shepherd, Jesus. And then I discovered, in our new church home, a Good Shepherd window over the altar, very similar in style and color to the one I'd left behind. It also, Sunday after Sunday, reminds me of the loving care of my Savior, who died for my sins. This illustrates for me that my Savior indeed goes with me wherever I am, in this world and in the next.

The main lesson of the widow's mite is not, however, the widow's generosity. In itself, it was a wonderful and generous gift,

Sulie

and from it we can learn a moral lesson, which is not only to be generous, but also to avoid clinging to the things of this world. But that certainly is not the most important part of this narrative—far from it. While the widow gave a great gift, it pales in comparison to the debt of sin she owed her Creator. Yes, she gave all she had to live on, but she still was a sinner in need of the generosity of her Savior, and what she gave was not enough to atone for her sin. And that's where we all find ourselves—in great need of our Savior's generosity, owing far more than we could ever pay.

The wonderful news for us is that our Lord is, indeed, generous. The widow gave all she had to live on, but Jesus gave His *life* for our sakes. The widow gave a little and it counted for much. The Savior gave all and it counted for everything; all of eternity is opened to us because of His gracious payment for sin. He gave all He could give—and He did it all for us.

Moving or facing any major life change, like a death in the family or a divorce, can force us to our knees, to rely on the generosity of God. Suffering has a way of bringing us to the point when we realize we can no longer cling to the things of this world and can cling to our Savior.

And in Christ, we truly find all that we need.

Prayer: Dear Lord Jesus, our Good Shepherd, thank You for Your reassurance that You provide all I need, and that in You, I have all the riches of heaven. Please help me in good and in difficult times to cling to You with strong faith, always trusting in Your goodness to save me. In Your name, I pray. **Amen.**

Julie

Personal Study Questions:
Psalm 49:6–9

1. "You can't buy your way out of trouble. You can't buy peace for others." So verses 7–9 seem to say. Still, we have been redeemed, ransomed, bought back. How is that possible? (See 1 Peter 1:18–19.)

2. What great blessing does Psalm 49:9 promise?

3. How does the forgiveness Jesus won for us help us with other problems that plague us here on earth?

Sulie

Psalm 49:10–15

Like sheep they are appointed for Sheol; death shall be their shepherd, and the upright shall rule over them in the morning. Their form shall be consumed in Sheol, with no place to dwell. But God will ransom my soul from the power of Sheol, for He will receive me. Selah

Baptized into Life

Everyone, it seems to me, has that epiphany, that moment of clarity when that youthful idea of immortality wears off. Obviously, we all know intellectually that we will someday die. But we live in denial, and the young do so especially. There are those times, however, when denial grows into a dawning realization that we, too, will die. Sometimes that realization comes as we age. Our bodies start to fall apart, and we know that someday, medication or treatment simply won't work. Or maybe we come to terms with our own mortality when someone close to us dies. We realize that if a loved one who seemed so strong, so full of life, died, then we will too. I realized that

Sulie

my life would one day come to an end when my maternal grand-mother died.

I was always close to Grammie. Some of my happiest child-hood memories come from time spent at her house in Boulder, Colorado. My grandfather died when I was fairly young. My one clear memory of him was sitting in his big chair and reading *The Poky Little Puppy* together. (I still love that book because of that lingering memory.)

But Grammie was different. I was closer to her partly be-cause she was in my life longer and partly because I spent more time with her. I remember afternoons in Grammie's kitchen with her and my mom, peeling, cutting, and cooking apples to make the best chunky applesauce ever. I have fond memories of playing card games and Yahtzee with her. And I remember the drive to her house in Boulder on Christmas Eve, listening to my brothers sing along to *"Feliz Navidad"* on the radio. When we'd arrive at Grammie's, we'd always open gifts and eat cream cheese cookies with red and green cherries on top.

Grammie died when I was a student in college. My fiancé and I flew to Colorado for the funeral. Seeing her, lifeless, in a padded coffin, made it all too real. Grammie had died. And it be-came quite clear that if she could die, I would die also.

Verses 10–12 in Psalm 49 focus on the truth that death lev-els the field. The wise and the foolish die, the rich and the poor die, grandmothers and granddaughters die. Death is the conse-quence of sin, and all alike are affected by it.

As a parish pastor's wife, I have seen over and over again the painful toll that affects a family devastated by a death. Families experienced not only the painful loss, but also the injus-tice of the young dying before the old, a baby dying before a single day outside the womb, or the feeling of uncertainty, of not know-ing what to do next when a spouse of fifty years dies suddenly.

Yet at these moments of tremendous loss, the love of God becomes a treasured jewel, a precious gift. The Gospel feels like a life preserver to a drowning man because in the face of death, there is only Christ to cling to. Money, reputation, even our clos-

Julie

est relationships cannot prevent the grave from taking its toll. "Man in his pomp will not remain" (v. 12a).

The writer of Psalm 49, inspired by the Holy Spirit, takes it a step further. Man must "leave [his] wealth to others" (v. 10b). That savings account we build up, the house we improve, the car we just paid off—all these things that seem important to us now do not go with us to the grave. We leave it all behind. Death separates the rich from their wealth and the poor from their poverty. Death levels the field. We all die. Yet, in Christ, the grave has no power over us. In Him, we have all the riches of heaven. In Him, we have the hope of eternal paradise.

The Gospel feels like a life preserver to a drowning man because in the face of death, there is only Christ to cling to. Money, reputation, even our closest relationships cannot prevent the grave from taking its toll.

Recently, two Christian friends and I were talking about funerals and which hymns we hope would be part of our own funeral services. I suggested "Lord, Thee I Love with All My Heart" (*LSB* 708). One of my favorite parts of this hymn is: "To Abr'ham's bosom bear me home, That I may die unfearing; And in its narrow chamber keep My body safe in peaceful sleep Until Thy reappearing" (st. 3). These words remind me that I do not need to fear the grave, although one of the most frightening things about death is imagining myself locked inside a coffin. Being claustrophobic no doubt feeds this fear, but it is a fear I need not have. For the Christian, there is no fear of the grave or the claustrophobia of the coffin or being buried in the earth. Jesus, our crucified Savior, has gone to the grave, was shrouded in burial clothes, and was sealed in a tomb. But the seal, the rock, the soldiers—even death itself—could not keep our Savior in the grave. Our Morning Star, our risen Lord, drained death of its power and the grave of its sting. This is why I like stanza 3 of "Lord, Thee I Love with All My Heart." The Lord *will* keep me safe, even through the perils of death and the narrow chamber of my coffin.

Verse 15 of Psalm 49 seems to me to be the climax of this psalm: "But God will ransom my soul from the power of Sheol, for

Julie

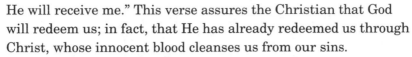

He will receive me." This verse assures the Christian that God will redeem us; in fact, that He has already redeemed us through Christ, whose innocent blood cleanses us from our sins.

After my grandmother died, I came to realize that I, too, will walk through the shadow of death. But I will not fear because Jesus, my crucified and risen Savior, will be with me every step of the way. You, a baptized child of God, also have this assurance: Christ has redeemed you, He has gone to the grave for you, and when you die, you will be brought to His loving arms to live in paradise forever.

Prayer: Dear Jesus, my crucified and risen Savior, thank You for Your sacrifice on the cross for my salvation. Thank You for going into the grave before me and for rising again on the third day. I thank You that You will redeem my life from the grave and that You will be with me even in death. Please help me to fear no evil, but always to trust in Your goodness to save me. Through Christ I pray. Amen.

Julie

thursday

Personal Study Questions: Psalm 49:10–15

1. Death acts as a "great leveler." How do verses 10–11 express that truth?

2. People today often express a yearning for meaning and purpose in their lives. If life on earth is all we have, how does death impact our yearning for meaning?

3. "Death shall be their shepherd" (v. 14a).

   a. Compare this fate of the wicked with those who know the Good Shepherd (Psalm 23; John 10).

   b. How does Psalm 49:15 point to the promise of eternal life that Jesus won for you?

4. How do the words of verses 12–15 help answer the writer's original "riddle," "Why should I fear in times of trouble?"

Psalm 49:16–20

Be not afraid when a man becomes rich, when the glory of his house increases. For when he dies he will carry nothing away; his glory will not go down after him. For though, while he lives, he counts himself blessed—and though you get praise when you do well for yourself—his soul will go to the generation of his fathers, who will never again see light. Man in his pomp yet without understanding is like the beasts that perish.

My Old Car

For the last several years, my husband and I have been the owners of a 1994 Geo Prizm, an old model that hasn't been manufactured since 2002. The car is our spare, and since I work at home and my husband is only about two blocks from his office, it's not really necessary that we have two cars in tip-top shape. The Prizm has always passed safety inspections, and we keep it tuned, but it definitely has some cosmetic issues, like rust along the rear fenders.

Overall, though, the car works just fine for quick trips to the local grocery store or wherever.

There are times, though, when I wish my old car weren't so old. I wish for a brand-new minivan with all the bells and whistles or an SUV with optional third-row seating. Wouldn't that make life better?

While on a recent vacation in Colorado, we had planned on renting a full-size car, but got bumped up to a minivan for the same rate. Oh, was it nice to spread out! During that vacation, we took a jeep tour in the mountains over rough terrain up to 12,500 feet. From the jeep, we saw the old stagecoach "road" that went straight up the side of the mountain near Salida, Colorado. Rocks the size of soccer balls were strewn all over this so-called road. It was hard for me to imagine *walking* over that rock-littered path, let alone driving a stagecoach over it. Yet, as challenging as life was 120 years ago, many intrepid souls braved the snow, the elevation, and the rustic traveling conditions to make a life for themselves and their families. Compared to this primitive and difficult way of life, my Geo Prizm seems like a limo. And the rented minivan? It was like an enchanted carriage!

The blessings of God are found in a Baby in a manger, in a Man hanging on a cross, in sins forgiven, in bread and wine, in the pages of Scripture. These are the riches God gives to us.

My point is that everything is relative. Compared to traveling conditions 120 years ago, I ride in absolute luxury in my climate-controlled, shock-absorbed, upholstered Geo Prizm. And compared to developing nations, my life—even with an aging car—is characterized by luxury, entertainment, and privilege.

The final verses of Psalm 49 exhort the reader to avoid becoming overwhelmed by the riches of others. So while I drive my well-used car around town, I should not covet what I do not have. Even further, I shouldn't become overwhelmed or afraid when someone else has more than I do. Don't we tend to think that the grass is greener on the other side of the fence? We see our friends' lives and wish we had the stuff they do or that our lives were easy and uncomplicated like theirs. But it's all a fantasy. Simply put,

Julie

coveting things or people or anything else separates us from the love of God. God has placed us amid the people He wants us to care for and in the situation where we can grow and learn more about Him. Coveting something other than what God has given not only makes us cranky and frustrated with life; it also separates us from Him.

An equally dangerous temptation is pointed out in verse 18, which says of the rich man, "For though, while he lives, he counts himself blessed—and though you get praise when you do well for yourself," and so on. The danger lies in equating "blessing" and "getting praise" with wealth and financial or material success. Don't we often do this, even subconsciously? When the bank account is fat with plenty of wiggle room, I think, even on a subconscious level, *Look how great we're doing. God must be blessing us. God is giving us all we need and more. How great am I!*

Certainly, God blesses the rich, for they would not have anything if it weren't for His provision, given through His generous hand. But God's Word also assures us that He blesses the poor, and the fact that a person lacks material wealth certainly doesn't mean God is withholding His blessing from her. As a matter of fact, in the Gospels, Jesus often gives warnings to the rich, such as Luke 18:25: "It is easier for a camel to go through the eye of a needle than for a rich person to enter the kingdom of God." And following the Beatitudes, Jesus warns, "But woe to you who are rich, for you have received your consolation. Woe to you who are full now, for you shall be hungry" (Luke 6:24–25). Such reversals characterize Christian theology. The humble and meek are exalted; the poor are blessed; the God of life dies on the cross for sins He did not commit.

The truth is that the Christian's treasure is hidden. It is not found in material wealth. It is not found in the square footage of that new house or the features on a new car. It is not found in things the eye can see. The blessings of God are found in a Baby in a manger, in a Man hanging on a cross, in sins forgiven, in bread and wine, in the pages of Scripture. These are the riches God gives to us. "But God, being rich in mercy, because of the

Julie

great love with which He loved us, even when we were dead in our trespasses, made us alive together with Christ—by grace you have been saved—and raised us up with Him and seated us with Him in the heavenly places in Christ Jesus, so that in the coming ages He might show the immeasurable riches of His grace in kindness toward us in Christ Jesus. For by grace you have been saved through faith. And this is not your own doing; it is the gift of God" (Ephesians 2:4–8). God forgives our sins, pardons our iniquities, and then bestows on us the riches of faith and eternal life with Him.

Eventually, we will replace our old Geo Prizm, but in the meantime, God is teaching me patience and contentment with what I have. Even more, however, God is blessing me bountifully with all the riches of heaven. Who could ask for anything more?

Prayer: Dear Lord, thank You for always bestowing upon me blessings I do not deserve. Thank You for Your kindness, which You have shown us in Christ. Help me, in rich days and poor, to trust in You for forgiveness, life, and salvation, knowing that my true treasure is in heaven. In Christ I pray. **Amen.**

Julie

Personal Study Questions:
Psalm 49:16–20

1. An old saying about the limitations of wealth's power to help goes something like this: "You never see a Wells Fargo truck following a hearse."

   a. With which verse from today's reading does this saying most closely correspond?

   b. Does this truth comfort, dismay, frustrate, or help you? Explain.

2. "Without understanding" (v. 20), we will always misplace life's priorities and find ourselves fearful in times of trouble (v. 5). What understandings protect us from this outcome?

3. How does today's faith narrative describe true wealth, true riches—regardless of the material blessings God may give us?

Group Bible Study for Week 4
Psalm 49

1. Psalm 49 is an instructional or "wisdom" psalm. Its intent is to teach. How are Psalm 1 and Psalm 49 alike in that regard?

2a. Why does the psalmist want everyone in the world (vv. 1–2) to hear his riddle and its solution (vv. 5–6)? What makes it so important that *both* rich and poor, the everyday person and the celebrity alike, grasp the truth presented here?

b. If you were to rephrase the riddle (vv. 5–6) in today's language so even those who never read the Bible would understand it, how would you put it?

c. When do people today ask this question? Explain.

3. It's hard enough to face trouble and turmoil. It's harder still when everyone around us seems ready to burst at the seams with blessings and when even cheaters seem to win (vv. 5–6, 18).

a. How does the psalmist describe the ungodly here on earth in verse 6? verse 11b? verse 12a? verse 13? verse 16? verse 18?
b. How does the psalmist describe the ungodly after life on earth ends in verse 10? verse 11a? verse 12b? verse 14? verse 17? verse 19? verse 20?

c. If we ask the riddle of verses 5–6 without remembering this contrast, anger, envy, and unbelief will likely fill our hearts. When you remember the contrast between now and eternity for the wicked, what thoughts and feelings arise in your heart instead?

4. Sometimes we ourselves act like the wicked. We are the cheaters of verse 5. We trust in our wealth, our possessions (vv. 6, 16), our land (v. 11), our reputation and the goodwill of other sinners like ourselves (v. 18).

a. How does the psalmist describe the future we deserve for our idolatry, sinful pride, and unbelief?

b. How do verses 7–9 and 15 speak Gospel ("Good News") to your heart as you consider your sins?

c. What does the incarnation of our Lord, His "enfleshment," have to do with our "ransom" (v. 15; see also Tuesday's faith narrative)?

5. In light of the truths of this psalm, how would you like your life from now on to be different? What will you ask the Holy Spirit to do *for* you and *in* you so those changes come about?

6. Which illustrations or insights from this week's faith narratives did you find especially meaningful or instructive? Explain.

Week Five

Psalm 73

¹ Truly God is good to ~~Israel,~~ *his church (in N.T.)*
to those who are pure in heart.
² But as for me, my feet had almost stumbled,
my steps had nearly slipped.
³ For I was envious of the arrogant
when I saw the prosperity of the wicked.
⁴ For they have no pangs until death;
their bodies are fat and sleek.
⁵ They are not in trouble as others are;
they are not stricken like the rest of mankind.
⁶ Therefore pride is their necklace;
violence covers them as a garment.
⁷ Their eyes swell out through fatness;
their hearts overflow with follies.
⁸ They scoff and speak with malice;
loftily they threaten oppression.
⁹ They set their mouths against the heavens,
and their tongue struts through the earth.
¹⁰ Therefore His people turn back to them,
and find no fault in them.
¹¹ And they say, How can God know?
Is there knowledge in the Most High?
¹² Behold, these are the wicked;
always at ease, they increase in riches.
¹³ All in vain have I kept my heart clean
and washed my hands in innocence.
¹⁴ For all the day long I have been stricken
and rebuked every morning.

¹⁵ If I had said, I will speak thus,
I would have betrayed the generation of your children.

¹⁶ But when I thought how to understand this,
it seemed to me a wearisome task,
¹⁷ until I went into the sanctuary of God;
then I discerned their end.

¹⁸ Truly You set them in slippery places;
You make them fall to ruin.
¹⁹ How they are destroyed in a moment,
swept away utterly by terrors!
²⁰ Like a dream when one awakes,
O Lord, when You rouse Yourself, You despise them as phantoms.
²¹ When my soul was embittered,
when I was pricked in heart,
²² I was brutish and ignorant;
I was like a beast toward You.

²³ Nevertheless, I am continually with You;
You hold my right hand.
²⁴ You guide me with Your counsel,
and afterward You will receive me to glory.
²⁵ Whom have I in heaven but You?
And there is nothing on earth that I desire besides You.
²⁶ My flesh and my heart may fail,
but God is the strength of my heart and my portion forever.

²⁷ For behold, those who are far from You shall perish;
You put an end to everyone who is unfaithful to You.
²⁸ But for me it is good to be near God;
I have made the Lord GOD my refuge,
that I may tell of all Your works.

Jane Wilke

Psalm 73:1–3

Truly God is good to Israel, to those who are pure in heart. But as for me, my feet had almost stumbled, my steps had nearly slipped. For I was envious of the arrogant when I saw the prosperity of the wicked.

A New Attitude

 grew up on a farm close to woods that were great for exploring. With brothers, sisters, and cousins, I enjoyed many day-long treks filled with fun and excitement. But there was one spot along the way that consistently brought fear to my heart. A creek cut through the woods, and to get from one side to the other, we had to take the precarious walk over a tree trunk

that had fallen across the deep ravine. Everyone else seemed to sail across with barely a stumble, but for me, it was a struggle. With my arms outstretched (picture a less-than-graceful tightrope walker) and my focus squarely on the goal ahead, I traversed the trunk, always in fear of slipping.

That's the picture that comes to mind as I read the first three verses of Psalm 73. Oh, how I can relate! My feet have nearly stumbled, my steps have nearly slipped. To call me a klutz would not be far from the truth. And as I absorb the words of the third verse, I find that they hit home through more than mere memories of treks in the woods. They cut deep into my heart.

In the third verse, we read, "For I was envious of the arrogant when I saw the prosperity of the wicked." There it is . . . the word that jabs at my heart: *envy*.

Have I ever been envious? Absolutely. And if you are being honest, you would have to agree that you have been too. We've all been there, haven't we?

Envy has been notoriously named as one of the seven deadly sins, and it would be easy to simply stop at that. In fact, you probably want me to stop because right now, you are most likely a bit uncomfortable with the topic. That's because envy is more than just a feeling; envy is an emotion, and a complex, puzzling one at that. It rears its ugly head when we see something that someone else has or when something good happens to someone else. It grows out of that insidious human tendency to assess how well we are doing by comparing ourselves to another person. Therefore, when we see something someone else has that we don't, we see it as a void in our lives. And the bigger the void we perceive, the more all-consuming the envy becomes.

I recall a college philosophy class in which Aristotle was discussed. I can picture the professor scrawling a quote from Aristotle across the board in huge letters: "Envy is pain at the good fortune of others." It really struck a chord (perhaps that's why I remember it so vividly).

Envy jabs at my heart because it causes all kinds of distress. While I feel guilty that I'm not happy for the person I envy, I also

Sane

risk being lead into disappointment, anger, and hurt. Can you relate? Is there one part of your life more than another where envy rears its ugly head? Returning to Psalm 73 to consider the depth of the psalmist's struggle, I realize even more how easily envy creeps in and the potentially destructive power it holds over me.

Envy is far from new. Its catastrophic nature has been around since Cain and Abel. It can indeed cause us to stumble and make our feet slip. Had I slipped off that log when I was a child, I most surely would have been hurt in the fall. And when I slip into envy, the same danger applies. Not only can envy lead to hurting others, as in the case of Cain, who killed his brother; it also has the potential to hurt me as it takes up residence in my very being.

Keeping my eyes firmly focused on the cross of Christ takes the focus off of me, where envy begins. Instead, I see the love and forgiveness of a Savior who will keep my feet from stumbling, my steps from slipping.

In Proverbs 14:30, we read that envy "makes the bones rot." I'm reminded of the story of a Native American grandfather who explained to his grandson that two wolves were at war inside him: Evil and Good. The wolf called Evil was characterized by envy, greed, arrogance, pride, and anger. Love, compassion, patience, and forgiveness characterized the wolf called Good.

"Which wolf will win?" asked the grandson.

"The one you feed," answered his grandfather.

How true it is! As much as we would like to package it some other way, we need to face the truth: envy is born of sin, and it leads to more sin. Envy is so closely tied to pride, bitterness, anger, and jealousy that it's hard to separate one from the others. We think that if we ignore it, it will go away. But it won't. Instead, it will manifest itself in other equally destructive ways. In 1 Peter 2:1, the apostle writes, "So put away all malice and all deceit and hypocrisy and envy and all slander."

Yet, left on our own, we cannot get rid of envy or any of its evil counterparts. They are part of our sinful nature, which places all sin beyond what any of us can do to destroy it. On our own, we are left to sin's destruction. But God the Father has had mercy upon us, not giving us what we truly deserve. Rather, He has showered grace upon us, giving us what we do not deserve: forgiveness through the death and resurrection of His Son, Jesus Christ, our Savior. With His arms stretched out upon the cross, Jesus took the punishment I deserve. And now, through Baptism, His death has become my death; His victory, my victory.

Through the gift of faith, new life in Christ is mine. It's a bit like the line in a song I once heard: "I have a new attitude." It was part of a musical in which a group of women looked at what was happening around them and realized their attitude was all in the way they looked at life. It's really no different here: it's time for me to realize that life is no longer about me; it's about Christ in me. And that changes everything. As we read in Galatians 5:24–26, "Those who belong to Christ Jesus have crucified the flesh with its passions and desires. If we live by the Spirit, let us also walk by the Spirit. Let us not become conceited, provoking one another, envying one another."

Does that mean envy will no longer threaten to make my feet stumble and my steps slip? No; sin remains real. But by God's grace, it no longer has the same power over me. My arms may have been stretched out for crossing that log of long ago, but the arms of Christ stretched out upon the cross move my focus away from the prosperity of the wicked toward living a life of gratitude that glorifies Him and Him alone. When my feet do slip, I live in the assurance that I can approach Him in confession and receive His forgiveness through His very own body and blood.

Is it easy to turn away from envy? No! Is it worth it? Absolutely! Keeping my eyes firmly focused on the cross of Christ takes the focus off of me, where envy begins. Instead, I see the love and forgiveness of a Savior who will keep my feet from stumbling, my steps from slipping. I can see with new eyes all the marvelous blessings He has bestowed upon me in love. They may not be the same as the perceived blessings of others, but in Christ, I will trust that He is enough!

My new attitude becomes that of gratitude—and a new gratitude that is focused on Christ is better than a new attitude any day!

Jane

Prayer: Dear Lord Jesus Christ, You know the sins that threaten to make me stumble and fall. Forgive me for those times when envy rises from deep within, causing me to take my focus off You. Help me to live by the Spirit and walk by the Spirit so that Your name may be glorified. **Amen.**

monday

Personal Study Questions:
Psalm 73:1–3

1. When we are "pure in heart" (v. 1), our hearts have a single focus— pleasing our Savior-God. Compare Matthew 5:8 and Matthew 23:23–24.

   a. On what were the religious leaders of Jesus' day, the scribes and Pharisees, focused? *tithing, appearance*

   b. Why did this draw a "woe" from Jesus? *They did not rely on him but on what they themselves did*

2. How does purity of heart contrast with envy, as today's faith narrative describes it?

3. "Israel" in Psalm 73 includes all who live by faith in the Messiah God sent and the forgiveness that flows from His sacrifice for our sins. It includes all who live in a covenant relationship with the God of Abraham, Isaac, and Jacob. (See Galatians 6:14–16.) In what ways is God "good to Israel" (v. 1)? to you as an individual member of His covenant nation?

Sane

Psalm 73:4–12

For they have no pangs until death; their bodies are fat and sleek. They are not in trouble as others are; they are not stricken like the rest of mankind. Therefore pride is their necklace; violence covers them as a garment.

Life Isn't Fair

Can't you just hear it now? The seven-year-old who determines that his half of the candy bar isn't as big as his sister's: "It's not fair!" The twelve-year-old who wants a cell phone because "all" of her friends have one, but you say no: "It's not fair!" The seventeen-year-old who can't go to the party because drugs and alcohol might be present: "It's not fair!"

And as the adult who finally loses her patience, can't you just imagine yourself saying (in a most exasperated tone), "Well, get used to it, because *life* isn't fair!"

Rewind with me for a moment to the struggles of Asaph, the author of Psalm 73. Verse 3 reveals his envy

Sane

152

as he looks around at the prosperity of the wicked. In the next few verses, he spells out precisely what he considers to be unfair. He characterizes the wicked, who prosper as greedy, oppressive, and haughty to the point that they openly ignore God. They seem to sail through life with few troubles. They make certain that everyone around them knows just how important they are. And they are downright mean and nasty to others. They seem to have it all, and, as icing on the cake, everything just seems to get better and better for them.

I don't know about you, but to me, that sounds a bit like the "in" crowd from high school. You know, the ones who seemed to have the looks, the clothes, the guys—everything the rest of us envied. I don't know what the current term is now (and I'm going to date myself here), but they were the "cool" kids—happy, carefree, popular.

Truthfully, when we were mature enough to look at things clearly, we most certainly didn't want to put others down or ride fast and loose or get in with the "wrong" crowd. But, boy, it was tempting. They really seemed to have it all, while the rest of us who were seemingly making the "better" decisions in life were left in the dust. It's not fair!

You'll notice that all the examples used thus far zero in on the young, the immature, as if to infer that we'll grow out of feeling that life isn't fair. Truth is, we don't, do we? Oh, the circumstances vary, but aren't we still tempted to fall into the trap of comparing what we have to what others have, and feeling like we always come up short?

It's hard not to. The world delivers the message that we can never be young enough, thin enough, or rich enough. While writing these devotions, I couldn't help but notice a commercial on TV—a teaser to get viewers to tune in to a feature story on how to "do more than just keep up with the Joneses." As you drive, you can hardly miss the commercials on radio for noninvasive ways to reshape your body or erase years from your face. And how many of us think that if we just lose those extra ten pounds, life will magically get better? We look at that friend who appears to be able to eat everything without putting on one ounce, and we think, *It's not fair!*

Then there's the co-worker who takes all the credit for a project we worked hard for, and she gets the promotion. Or the friend with whom you shared a confidence who turns it into spiteful gossip, yet seems to have everyone as her best friend. Or the neighbor who openly cheats on her taxes, then waves as she drives by in her new BMW convertible.

When you and I fall into the trap of thinking that we deserve better or shouldn't be treated this way or that, it will be because our focus is in the wrong place. . . . But when Christ died on the cross, it was "just [as] if I'd" died—that's what we mean when we say we have been justified *through Christ.*

Can you feel it? Can you relate to the tension and struggle within Asaph? Can you see how he might have difficulty with the sharp contrast between the carefree, often prosperous life of evildoers and his own angst as a godly, God-fearing man? It's not fair!

When you think about it, though, how much of what we consider unfair is all about us thinking we deserve better? It's as if we have set up a scenario for how our life was—or is—supposed to be and we are waiting for God to comply. And when He doesn't, we tell ourselves that it's just not fair.

Well, here it comes, that age-old response: life isn't fair! But let me offer that response with a twist: life isn't fair, and that's a very good thing. After all, if life were tit-for-tat, even-steven, quid pro quo, there'd be someone, somewhere, keeping a scorecard. And if left up to us, we'd fall far short.

In Romans 3:23, we read, "For all have sinned and fall short of the glory of God." When the apostle Paul wrote about God's glory in this verse, he was referring to God's intent at creation, when He created man in His own image, in all holiness and righteousness. But that was before the fall into sin, before there was any reason to keep score, before there would ever be a winner or a loser. Because of sin, we are eternally separated from God. If there were a scorecard, every sin we have ever committed in thought or in word or in deed would have been marked against us.

In all fairness, we'd lose big-time! Because of sin, we would

Sane

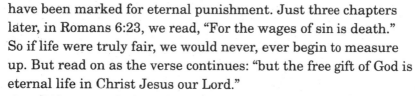

have been marked for eternal punishment. Just three chapters later, in Romans 6:23, we read, "For the wages of sin is death." So if life were truly fair, we would never, ever begin to measure up. But read on as the verse continues: "but the free gift of God is eternal life in Christ Jesus our Lord."

Did you catch that? Being returned to a right state with God is a gift. It has nothing to do with our effort and everything to do with the sacrificial love of our Savior. If there were anyone who would have had the right to shout "It's not fair!" it would have been God's very own Son, Jesus Christ, as He carried our sins to the cross. I can only imagine the pain as He cried out, "My God, My God, why have You abandoned Me?" God turned His back on Jesus when He *should* have been turning His back on me. No, life isn't fair. And it's a good thing.

So now it's time to flip the switch from thinking too highly of ourselves to having the servant heart of Christ. Paul continues in Philippians 2:5–8: "Have this mind among yourselves, which is yours in Christ Jesus, who, though He was in the form of God, did not count equality with God a thing to be grasped, but made Himself nothing, taking the form of a servant, being born in the likeness of men. And being found in human form, He humbled Himself by becoming obedient to the point of death—even death on a cross."

Did you catch that? He humbled Himself for me; He humbled Himself for you. When you and I fall into the trap of thinking that we deserve better or shouldn't be treated this way or that, it will be because our focus is in the wrong place. It will be because we think that life is all about us. But when Christ died on the cross, it was "just [as] if I'd" died—that's what we mean when we say we have been *justified* through Christ. We are united with Him in Baptism; therefore, His death becomes our death, and we are made just, or right, with God because the debt for our sin has been paid.

Therefore, being united with Christ, we have a new attitude. We will "look not only to [our] own interests, but also to the interests of others" (Philippians 2:4), keeping in mind that because

Christ was united to us in sin and guilt, we are now united with Him to serve others.

No, life isn't fair. And because of Christ, I can be glad.

Prayer: Dear God, heavenly Father, forgive me for all the times I've thought that life was all about me, for it is in those times that my focus falls away from You. Pour out Your Holy Spirit upon me so my focus remains fixed on You and Your gift of amazing grace. In the name of Your Son, my Savior, I pray. Amen.

tuesday

Personal Study Questions:
Psalm 73:4–12

1. When are you tempted to bemoan the fact that "life is not fair"? As you reflect on today's faith narrative, why are you glad it's not?

   Its made me more thankful for what I have

2. In what ways does today's assigned passage from Psalm 73 remind you of Psalms 37 and 49?

3. How does the Lord's goodness to the wicked lead them ever more deeply into sin?

   They figure the can do as they please and reap the benefits

4. When has God used troubles and challenges in your own life to drive you into the Holy Scriptures and, thus, closer to Himself?

   Probably when my middle son was born

5. Based on your answers to questions 3 and 4, what do you deduce about human definitions of "good" and "bad" circumstances?

   It all depends on how you look at it and what you learn from it

Sane

Psalm 73:13–17

All in vain have I kept my heart clean and washed my hands in innocence. For all the day long I have been stricken and rebuked every morning. If I had said, "I will speak thus," I would have betrayed the generation of your children. But when I thought how to understand this, it seemed to me a wearisome task, until I went into the sanctuary of God; then I discerned their end.

The Rest of the Story

I love to watch the Olympics. Perhaps because I am the consummate nonathlete, I live vicariously through these highly skilled, well-trained, truly disciplined athletes. Perhaps it's precision I most admire because my favorite competitions are gymnastics and skating. I used to tune in each night these events were broadcast to watch in anticipation. I'd wonder, *Will she score that perfect 10 on the uneven bars or execute the triple axel without falling?* I'd watch with the rest of the world to see how the story ended.

Sane

But times have changed. Now, because we live in the age of instant information, we no longer have to wait—we can go online and see the faces of the gold-, silver-, and bronze-medal winners even before the broadcast. We already know before watching how the story ends.

That also means, of course, that in addition to seeing who is rejoicing in victory, we also see who is suffering the agony of defeat. Believe it or not, as we progress through Psalm 73, we see that same thing happen to Asaph. He gets a peek at how the story ends, and he discovers who will win and who will be defeated.

Asaph has watched and agonized over how those he characterizes as wicked flaunt their carefree lifestyle, laced with success. We see the envy that has slowly seeped into his entire being evidenced in bitterness. Emotional intensity jumps off the page as we read how Asaph wonders if God even cares. It's as if he's ready to give up on the whole thing. He struggles because he can't say anything—venting about this would surely be a betrayal.

So, what does he do? Verse 17 tells us that he enters the sanctuary of God. I'm going to assume that the sanctuary he entered was God's temple. After all, he is a musician. We discover in 1 Chronicles 16:4–7 that he was one of the Levite clan designated to lead in singing and playing instruments. In 2 Chronicles 29:30, he is also mentioned as "Asaph the seer," which makes me wonder if people saw him as someone who could see beyond face value. When he was out in the midst of the chaos, when all he could see was the prosperity of the wicked, he was caught up in bitterness. He was a musician who loved harmony, but all he could see was discord. Yet when he escaped the cacophony and went into the sanctuary of God, he saw loud and clear what would happen to the wicked: they would be defeated.

Do you recall the line for which commentator Paul Harvey is best known? "And now, the *rest* of the story . . ." I can just imagine Asaph quietly playing his instruments. I can see him closing his eyes as he recalled the stories of God's faithfulness to his ancestors. And I can just imagine God sitting him down in the quiet of His house and saying, "Now, Asaph, for the *rest* of the story . . ."

Sane

Asaph was led to see that everything he perceived as success for the wicked was entirely fleeting. It was temporary. Without warning, it could be swept away. But what God offered was eternal. His faithfulness, His love—*that* would be forever.

We can't close off the world entirely, but through His Spirit at work within us, we begin to see things in a new light. We test what is happening today against what we know to be the end of the story. It's a story that ends in victory.

What discord is in your life? What cacophony is drowning out what God would say to you today? You and I have a great advantage over Asaph. He lived in the days of King David, before God's rescue of Daniel from the den of lions and the three men from the fiery furnace. He lived centuries before God's ultimate rescue of us through the gift of His Son, born in humility as both God and man. Centuries before God's Son would live the perfect life we cannot. Centuries before God's Son would take our sins to the cross and then rise again in glory. Centuries before He would ascend into heaven with the words "And behold, I am with you always, to the end of the age" (Matthew 28:20).

Yes, through God's Word and the gift of faith He has worked in our hearts, we know the rest of the story. The question is, are we embracing it? Or are we focusing on what's wrong in our lives rather than on what's right? Do you need to enter the sanctuary of God to be brought back to the end of the story? I know that I do.

I remember a children's message given at church some time ago (I especially remember it because chocolate was involved) where the pastor used an M&M's dispenser and a bag of the candies. He showed the children that whatever you pour in is precisely what comes out. If chocolate candies go in, then chocolate candies come out. He went on to say that whatever we surround ourselves with—the books we read, the friends we keep, the things we watch on television—all feeds into the way we look at the world. They affect what we think and say and do. But if we surround ourselves with God and His Word, we will test what we see and hear to discover how to look at the world with a focus that sees what's right because God is good.

That's not so far off from what happens when we enter God's

Sane

sanctuary. We can't close off the world entirely, but through His Spirit at work within us, we begin to see things in a new light. We test what is happening today against what we know to be the end of the story.

It's a story that ends in victory, and that's the hope to which we cling. That means that no matter what happens to me today—whether I slip while trying a triple axel or lose my grip on the uneven parallel bars—it will all be okay because although I suffer defeats along the way, I will see eternal victory as I cling to Christ in faith.

Have you given any thought to where your sanctuary might be? Is it in your faith community where you can be surrounded by others who also come to confess their brokenness and hear the words of forgiveness, where we are drawn ever closer to God through His Word, and where we can touch and taste forgiveness in the body and blood of Christ?

Is it in the quiet of your home where you can open God's Word to listen to what He might speak to your heart? Is it in the wonder of His creation as you gaze upon miracle after miracle and consider the words of the psalmist in Psalm 95:3–7: "For the LORD is a great God, and a great King above all gods. In His hand are the depths of the earth; and the heights of the mountains are His also. The sea is His, for He made it, and His hands formed the dry land. Oh come, let us worship and bow down; let us kneel before the LORD, our Maker! For He is our God, and we are the people of His pasture, and the sheep of His hand"?

Or perhaps Psalm 46:10: "Be still, and know that I am God." Or even Psalm 100:3: "Know that the LORD, He is God. It is He who made us, and we are His."

Even more so than Asaph did, we know the rest of the story. Sit with God's Word and slowly read Hebrews 11. It's one of my favorites because in it, I can see the hand of God's faithfulness through all generations. It starts with these words: "Now faith is the assurance of things hoped for, the conviction of things not seen" (v. 1); and it chronicles the stories of how God's faithful passed through the trials of life, keeping their eyes focused on

Sane

God's promise.

It ends with these words: "All these, though commended through their faith, did not receive what was promised, since God had provided something better for us, that apart from us they should not be made perfect" (vv. 39–40).

And that perfection is be found only in and through Christ. Escape to God's sanctuary, for it is there that we learn the rest of the story.

Prayer: Lord God, heavenly Father, lead me to Your sanctuary where You reveal to me the rest of the story, the story of victory through Your Son, my Savior, Jesus Christ. Clear away the clutter that I may hear only the sounds of Your love to me. In Jesus' name I pray. Amen.

Sane

Personal Study Questions:
Psalm 73:13–17

1. How does the psalmist's lot in life (vv. 13–17) contrast with that of the wicked (vv. 4–12)?

2. When have you and the psalmist thought a lot alike (vv. 13–17)? How might this indicate impurity of heart (v. 1)?

3. Verse 14 reads, "For all the day long I have been stricken and rebuked every morning." In what way can we think of the Lord's rebuke as a great blessing? *It makes us thankful for what we have*

4. Where does the psalmist find answers to his questions and relief for his guilt? Where do you? (See v. 17.)

   in the sanctuary of God

Psalm 73:18–24

Truly You set them in slippery places; You make them fall to ruin. How they are destroyed in a moment, swept away utterly by terrors! Like a dream when one awakes, O Lord, when You rouse Yourself, You despise them as phantoms. When my soul was embittered, when I was pricked in heart, I was brutish and ignorant; I was like a beast toward You. Nevertheless, I am continually with You; You hold my right hand. You guide me with Your counsel, and afterward You will receive me to glory.

Mood Swing

Mood swings—they follow us through life, don't they? Think of the two-year-old who is the living epitome of the "terrible twos." Simply growing into his own sense of autonomy, he tests all boundaries and every limit of your patience; yet you continue to love him without condition.

Sane

Fast-forward to adolescence and into the teenage years. At what precise moment did your thirteen-year-old become an entirely different person? and who will she be today? As you live through the roller coaster of unpredictable emotions, you know that this, too, shall pass; and you continue to love her without condition.

And, well, we won't even go into the rest of the mood swings that follow us through the continuing stages of life—we'll gloss right over them because, no matter which stage you and I are in, we know them all too well. Suffice it to say that whenever we experience one of our own dreaded mood swings, it's wonderful to be surrounded by people who love us without condition.

So far in Psalm 73, we've seen Asaph's moods swing from envy to bitterness to quiet reflection. Now we see his mood swing to introspection. He's in the "oh, my goodness, I've been a beast" mode. We can just imagine the thoughts running through his mind: *How could I have been so self-centered? What do I have to complain about anyway? If I could, I'd take it all back. I should have known better. It would serve me right if God decided that He'd had enough with me and my complaining!*

In my mind, I'm seeing a scene from a movie or TV show—I can't remember which one right now—in which a guy is beating his head against a doorframe and muttering, "Stupid! Stupid! Stupid!" Asaph calls himself a senseless, ignorant, brutish beast. Maybe that's his version of what to mutter as he's beating his head against the wall of regret.

Fortunately, his story (and ours) doesn't end here. Without skipping a beat, Asaph moves to wonderment at how, through it all, God has not turned His back on him. The note in my *Concordia Self-Study Bible* for Psalm 73:23–26 says it all: "Although he had (almost) fallen to the level of beastly stupidity, God has not, will not, let him go—ever!"

What words of comfort these are to me! How many times have I been so self-centered that I could see only what was wrong with my life, not what was right? How many times have I looked at some life situation and treated it like climbing a mountain, with the focus on how far I have left to go, instead of how far, with God's guidance, I've already come? How many times have I wondered if that person I hurt—much less God—could ever forgive me?

Sometimes we get stuck in the mode of regret. We don't know how long Asaph was stuck, as I imagine this psalm was written in retrospect, maybe even as a song to share as a musician. Yet he must have been stuck long enough for it to merit a mention. Maybe that's because he can appreciate even more the depth of God's love when he sees how much he doesn't deserve it.

The more we stay stuck, the more we block the peace that is ours from Christ. That's what happens when it's all about us. But when it becomes about what Christ did for us, the sun (or, shall I say, Son) then shines through the doom and gloom.

Maybe there's something of significance here for us as well. As confessing Christians, we live each day as both saint and sinner. What is laid out before us in these verses becomes a helpful visual for our own ongoing tension between the two. Another way to put it would be to call this a tension between Law and Gospel within us. Each is distinct from the other, but they are connected in a symmetrical sort of way. Both are found in God's Word, and both point us to Christ. But without one we cannot really understand the other. Allow me to explain.

Simply put, the Law points me to my sin and helps me realize my own personal need for a Savior. It shines the light on my unworthiness as I realize, time and again, that I continuously let God down by what I think, what I say, and what I do. In other words, the Law convicts me and locks me in a prison of guilt. It points me to Christ because on my own, I will never, *ever* get it right.

Then comes the Gospel—the indescribably incredible Good News that despite my unworthiness and imperfection, God sent His only beloved Son to live the holy, perfect life I could not (and cannot) and to carry my sins to the cross. There He was crucified, taking the punishment I deserved. There He died for my sins . . . for your sins . . . for the sins of every person who has walked the earth.

Sane

Despite me, God sent Jesus for me. He has unlocked the prison of my guilt. In Colossians 2:13–15, we read: "And you, who were dead in your trespasses and the uncircumcision of your flesh, God made alive together with Him, having forgiven us all our trespasses, by canceling the record of debt that stood against us with its legal demands. This He set aside, nailing it to the cross. He disarmed the rulers and authorities and put them to open shame, by triumphing over them in Him."

Without the Law, I would not fully realize how much I needed, and still need, Christ. And without the Gospel, I would still be locked in that prison, stuck in that rut. But as I confess my sins, I live in the confidence that through Christ and because of Christ, I am forgiven. When I cling to Him in faith, I live in the assurance that "neither death nor life, nor angels nor rulers, nor things present nor things to come, nor powers, nor height nor depth, nor anything else in all creation, will be able to separate us from the love of God in Christ Jesus our Lord" (Romans 8: 38b–39).

As we bring our focus back to Asaph, we see a microcosm of the same—he did not yet know how Christ would come, but he had once again been reminded of God's great goodness and love. He could look back to see how God had guided him through the stumbles and around the pitfalls. And he could look ahead to the promise of God guiding him to glory.

Are you stuck in a rut, living in regret over something you know you should not have said or done or thought? Are you beating your head against the proverbial wall of regret, saying, "Stupid, stupid, stupid"? Are you locked in a prison today from which you need release? Know that Jesus is that release. Cling to Him in faith as a loved, redeemed, forgiven child of God.

God, through Christ, has unlocked the prison, but have you walked through the door He has opened for you? Just like when we sometimes choose to stay in that bad mood until we are good and ready to let it go, we cannot see how much time we are wasting by staying stuck in the muck. The more we stay stuck, the more joy we prevent from seeping into our very being. The more we stay stuck, the more we block the peace that is ours from

Sane

Christ. That's what happens when it's all about us. But when it becomes about what Christ did for us, the sun (or, shall I say, Son) then shines through the doom and gloom.

Oh—there's one more thing: remember that no matter which direction your mood swings, God will love you through it all, and He will not give up on you. Bask with the psalmist in rediscovering that God loves us in spite of us. That's what Christ is all about.

Prayer: Dear Father, sometimes we just don't get it. We see the blessings You hold out to us, but we get so focused on how we don't deserve them that we forget what Christ did to win them for us. Forgive us, and renew in our hearts a sense of gratitude for Your great gifts of grace. Through Jesus Christ, Your Son, our Lord. **Amen.**

Personal Study Questions:
Psalm 73:18–24

1. Asaph's mood has shifted from envy to bitterness to quiet reflection and, now, to self-examination. He seemingly beats his head against a wall of regret. What sins does he confess in verses 21–22? When have you been guilty of these same sins? *bitterness*

2. Although our hearts are far from pure (v. 1), our position before God is not precarious, as is that of the wicked (vv. 18–20). Why not? (Look ahead to vv. 21–26 and consider the insights from today's faith narrative.) *We will fall occasionally and he will pick us up*

3. How does Colossians 2:13–15 reinforce the Gospel message for you today? *Christ died for all our sins*

Sane

Psalm 73:25–28

Whom have I in heaven but You? And there is nothing on earth that I desire besides You. My flesh and my heart may fail, but God is the strength of my heart and my portion forever. For behold, those who are far from You shall perish; You put an end to everyone who is unfaithful to You. But for me it is good to be near God; I have made the Lord GOD my refuge, that I may tell of all Your works.

God Is Enough

Storms. What visual comes to mind as you read the word *storm*? Perhaps you've lived through a blizzard or two, with snow blowing fiercely across the plains, socking you in for days. Or maybe you recall a tornado that lasted mere moments, but wiped away a lifetime of hard work and memories. Or maybe you've never had to weather any drastic storms, but you know all too well the typical thunderstorm, where the fronts collide, the clouds build, the winds blow, the thunder booms, and the lightning flashes.

Sane

170

I will confess to being a Weather Channel geek—I'm fascinated by weather, storms in particular. As I find myself reading the last few verses of Psalm 73, I can't help but see parallels to a storm. The first verses are dark; the skies are overcast. Then the light breaks through and the psalm ends in full sunlight. It goes from emotional intensity to reflection to thanksgiving. Not too far from our own lives, is it?

Storms are a fact of life. There is no escaping the sometimes violent shifts in weather patterns; neither is it possible to escape the storms life brings our way. Life's storms come in all shapes and sizes: serious illness, accidents, job loss, crumbling relationships, loneliness, addictions, and financial crisis, to name a few. Some build over time, while others come suddenly—but all threaten to destroy our sense of peace and calm.

At the risk of sounding like a cliché, it's not the storm itself that shatters, but how we come through the storm that matters. Tall, mature oak trees look impressive, not because they've survived the calm, but because they've survived the storms. As the winds shake and the rains beat down, the oak develops its rugged fibers, becoming stronger with each storm.

Many people wish for a life that is protected and easy. After all, our world promotes an "I want it easy" and "I want it now" kind of life. But that's not reality, is it? And when I think about it, I can't help but wonder, would that even be good?

Some of the people I admire most are those in whom I have witnessed strength as they faced adversity. The storms didn't destroy them; the storms shaped them, a bit like that strong oak. To the world, they may not look particularly impressive, but when you look closely, you see strength, grace, and wisdom. That's how I want to be when I grow up, and it won't happen without some storms.

Some believe that if you are "truly Christian," life will be perfect—no storms, no troubles, no hurt. No way! The truth is that Satan is most threatened by those who firmly cling to Christ. Therefore, he works overtime to make them his targets. It's been said that if we call ourselves Christian but have no struggles in life, then Satan must not be very worried about us.

What's so amazing is how God uses the storms and struggles that come our way to shape us, enabling us to be even stronger witnesses to His glory. In verse 28, we find the psalmist proclaiming that God is his refuge. The definition of the word *refuge* leads us to God as Asaph's source of protection and shelter in the storms of life. That doesn't mean that the storms will stop coming; it means that even as they continue to rage around him, they will not destroy him. Neither will they destroy me—or you—if we tap into God's strength rather than our own.

Some would believe that if you are "truly Christian," life will be perfect—no storms, no troubles, no hurt. No way! The truth is that Satan is most threatened by those who firmly cling to Christ. Therefore, he works overtime to make them his targets.

Asaph weathered a storm that threatened his faith as he looked around him at the prosperity of the wicked. Had he stayed focused on the torment his envy produced, he would have been consumed by the storm. He was ready to give up on God, but God did not give up on him. God led him to a new understanding. And in the end, the storm blew over and the light dawned as he realized anew God's counsel, God's presence, and God's power.

I find it interesting that the word *heart* (or *hearts*) is used six times in this psalm. Today we think of the heart as the center of our emotions. (Remember when we used to sign those little love notes with an "I ♥ you"?) But in the Hebrew language and culture, it referred to the center of the person: the disposition, the character, the thought process. In other words, it's more about thinking and less about feeling.

I know, I know—that kind of goes against the grain of how a woman is put together; after all, we are known more for ruling with our hearts than with our heads. But this train of thought makes sense here as it helps us to see that Asaph's whole self, not just his feelings, were wrapped up in the torment of the storm. It affected his whole being, physically, emotionally, and spiritually. And as he considered the entire situation, he was led to the sanctuary, the refuge, of God's love. He was reminded anew that "when I can't count on anything else in life, O, Lord, I can count on You!"

I see yet another parallel in the story of Jesus with His disciples on the Sea of Galilee. We find three accounts of this story: Matthew 8:23–27, Mark 4:35–41, and Luke 8:22–25. It's the one commonly referred to as "the stilling of the storm." If you aren't familiar with it, I urge you to read it.

I find it curious that all three Gospels place this event shortly after Jesus had used parables to teach about faith. We can assume that the disciples who got into the boat with Jesus were also present with Him as He taught. Here they were, unexpectedly thrust into a storm, with the winds raging and the waves threatening. Yet Jesus slept. The torment of their fear overtook them, and as they woke Jesus, they had but one question: "Don't You care if we drown?" And what did Jesus do? He rebuked the winds and the waves, and they were surrounded by quiet and calm. The disciples were amazed. What they had repeatedly heard and held as head knowledge now touched their hearts, and they said, "Who is this? Even the wind and the waves obey Him!"

Rewind to Asaph and see the same progression from the torment of the storm to the quiet of reflection to new awareness of God's power. I am inclined to wonder how many times that same thing has happened to me. How many times has it happened to you? How many times have the winds and waves led us to the point of desperation, perhaps even anger at God or doubting His power and presence? How many times have we thought He didn't care? Yet, in the midst of it all, how many times have we not gone to Him in prayer, not asked Him to help, while knowing that He will?

To me, that's the key: knowing that He will. I am less amazed that Jesus calmed the sea and more amazed at His complete confidence in God the Father. He was so confident that even in the middle of a storm, He could rest His head and fall asleep. He knew it would all be okay.

In the midst of our storms, do we know in our heart of hearts that we can approach God the Father with the same confidence, knowing that He is ultimately in control and will calm the storm in one way or another? It might not be in quite the way we expect, but we can most surely trust that the will of God is perfect for us. After all, the fear that torments us is born in sin—the same sin that God sent His Son to triumph over, the same sin that Christ our Savior took to the cross, the same sin that now stands for-given because of Christ's body and blood.

The psalm ends with a declaration: "But for me, it is good to be near God." Perhaps another way to say that is "But as for me, whatever the storm, God in Christ is enough!"

Prayer: Dear God, heavenly Father, in the midst of difficult moments, help me to seek only You. In the midst of quiet moments, teach me to listen for You. In the midst of every moment, lead me to trust in You. For You are my refuge and strength. In the name of Your Son, my Savior and Redeemer, I pray. **Amen.**

Sane

Personal Study Questions:
Psalm 73:23–28

1. While most of the rest of the psalm has filled our hearts with
   warnings, threats, and accusations (Law), verses 23–26 proclaim the
   sweetest Gospel. What gifts of God's grace does the psalmist detail
   in these verses? When have you experienced each of these?
   guidance and the promise to be with him

2. How does relying on each of these gifts from God protect us from
   the dangers unbelievers must face on their own?

3. The last two verses (vv. 27–28) form a fitting summary and conclusion to the psalm. How so?

Group Bible Study for Week 5
Psalm 73

1. What insights have you gained in the past five weeks as you studied the contrasts the psalmists make between those who belong to God and those who reject Him? With what problems, questions, or troubles have these insights helped you?

2. Suppose you were to outline this psalm and give each section a title. How would you divide it? What title and subtitles would you use?

3. How is Psalm 73 like Psalms 37 and 49? How does it differ?

4. Explain the psalmist's description of himself in verse 22. In what ways do envy, unbelief, and impurity of heart make us "like beasts"—less than the fully human, joyful, serving people our Creator-God intended?

5. Compare verse 15 with verse 28.

   a. In verse 15, how would the psalmist have framed his words of witness, his testimony?

   b. As the psalm ends, to what will he witness?

   c. When has discouragement, envy, or even despair damaged your witness?

   d. How does it comfort you to know that God in Christ is your refuge (verse 28)?

   e. How could keeping the truths of verse 28 in mind help your witness remain strong and positive into the future?

~~~~~~

6. Compare verses 1 and 28.

    a. How would the "wicked" (vv. 4–12) define "good"?
    money, job, position, good works

    b. How does the psalmist define it as his poem of praise concludes?
    knowledge of God

    c. How do you define it in light of Psalms 37, 49, and 73? Explain.

    d. What will you say to your Lord about that? *Thank you*

7. Friday's faith narrative contrasts "feeling" and "knowing." What insights
from this contrast could help you the next time you find yourself trapped
in a storm of frustration or fear?

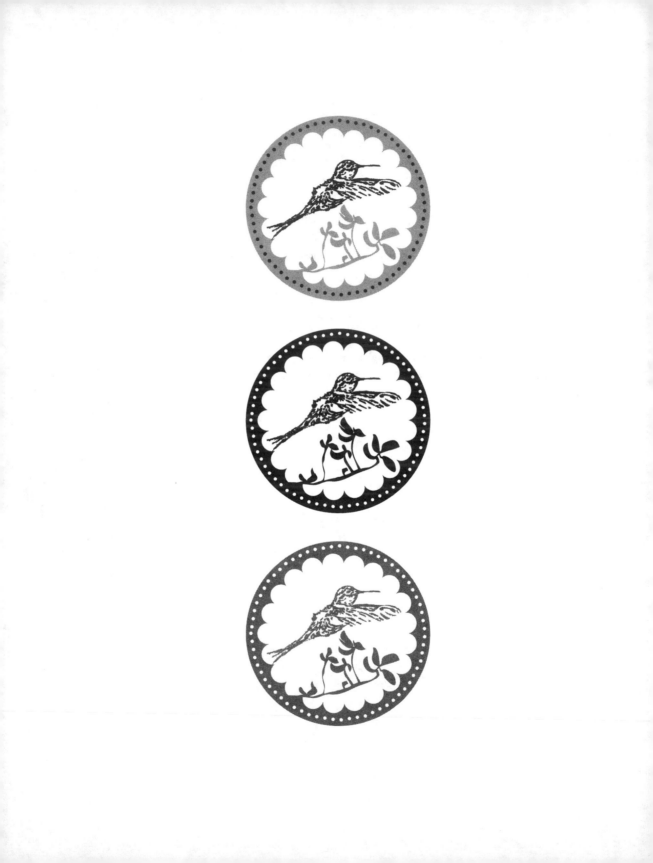

Week Six

Psalm 111

[1] Praise the LORD!
I will give thanks to the LORD with my whole heart,
in the company of the upright, in the congregation.
[2] Great are the works of the LORD,
studied by all who delight in them.
[3] Full of splendor and majesty is His work,
and His righteousness endures forever.
[4] He has caused His wondrous works to be remembered;
the LORD is gracious and merciful.
[5] He provides food for those who fear Him;
He remembers His covenant forever.
[6] He has shown His people the power of His works,
in giving them the inheritance of the nations.
[7] The works of His hands are faithful and just;
all His precepts are trustworthy;
[8] they are established forever and ever,
to be performed with faithfulness and uprightness.
[9] He sent redemption to His people;
He has commanded His covenant forever.
Holy and awesome is His name!
[10] The fear of the LORD is the beginning of wisdom;
all those who practice it have a good understanding.
His praise endures forever!

Ruth Koch

Psalm 111:1

Praise the LORD! I will give thanks to the LORD with my whole heart, in the company of the upright, in the congregation.

With All My Heart

ome to church with a pastor's wife. It's a trip! I've been attending church most of my life, but I've been going to church as a pastor's wife for forty years. Every week. Rain or shine. Snowstorm or no storm. With kids and without. Willingly or not. An intensely private person in a public role. Who would notice if I weren't there? Everyone!

For me, the morning service actually begins in the parking lot. Brothers and sisters in Christ disembarking from their cars and vans and trucks. Time to wave and smile and give the single mom a hand with the toddlers. In the early years, with my husband already at work for hours, I appreciated the grace and friendliness of that helping hand with my toddlers. Now I can return the love with interest.

Making my way up the steps and into the building has never proved easy. My arms, when not filled with our two little girls, were filled with envelopes addressed to fellow members and books to return or hand out and countless other items from our life together: a casserole dish, boots for the Schrams' kids, a newspaper article for a fellow counselor, notes to myself about whom to see about what, an armful of fabric for new banners. In later years, my arms were full of adult class materials, books, handouts, and overhead transparencies. Up the steps and into the narthex.

The narthex is the congregation's living room. In many ways, these folks are my guests, greeted with warmth and love and sometimes a hug. "What happened with your mom's surgery?" "How is your son doing in his new school?" "Does your sister like college?" "How are your parents getting along in London?" And all the time, I'm trying to deliver the envelopes, present the books, and find the new owners of the boots. Each person is the only person, yet my eyes must keep moving, my attention focused, my alertness high. Who's there? Who's not?

Only a few minutes before the worship service begins, Tamara approaches me, anxiety scrunching up her face. I hear her story, listening to the "short version," as she calls it; I also hear the organist begin the prelude and know I have to get myself into the sanctuary within a reasonable time. I promise Tamara a phone call and pledge my prayers for her and her family. A quick hug and I propel myself into the sanctuary, purposefully ignoring those who went to the early service and would also like a word with me before they head home. It's taken a long time, but I've finally admitted that I can't be in two places at once.

By the time I'm seated, the first hymn has already begun. Jokingly referred to as "the late Ruth Koch," I've managed again to get there *almost* on time. *Now, Self, focus! Where are you and what are you doing? Apply yourself to worship.* But first I jot a reminder on the back of the service folder to call Tamara on Monday. Juggling the service folder and the hymnal and looking around to see who my worship neighbors are, I finally breathe and sing. I'm not a good singer, but I have learned how important it is to *just sing* and enter into the heart of the worshiping community by setting aside self-consciousness and pride. It's a hymn of praise, and I do believe that the Lord inhabits the praise of His people. Christ is present. The music unites us and allows us to express our faith—and actually builds our faith and our community of Christ.

There's a special intimacy in sharing the peace of God, looking into a person's eyes, and saying by handshake and smile, "This peace is for you." It's one of the joys of being part of the Body of Christ.

I'm almost totally into worship until the sermon. Argh! Don't get me wrong; I love my husband's preaching, and over the years, he has just gotten better and better. But I have some learning to do to separate myself from him and what he says and does when he's in the pulpit. A member once told me that she just loves to watch my face while I listen to my husband preach: such adoration! I can't believe I've been projecting adoration all these years when I am actually a mass of anxiety and suspense on the inside. Here's what's running through my anxious mind: *No! Don't use that example! . . . I never thought of it that way before! . . . I think it's getting to be a bit too long. . . . Wow, that was a great point! I hope Bob-who-always-takes-notes has jotted that one down! . . . I know it took courage to speak that word from God, but that is sure going to ruffle feathers!*

When the sermon is over, I exhale—and realize that despite my agitation, I have learned and grown. David's done it again: courageous and exemplary preaching can even reach me in my gnarled-up state!

Now we exchange the peace of the Lord, and I want to share that peace with as many people as I can reach, especially the children. I look 'em square in the eye and say, "The peace of the Lord be yours." The adults will have to wait a moment or two. There's a special intimacy in sharing the peace of God, looking into a per-

Ruth

son's eyes, and saying by handshake and smile, "This peace is for *you*." It's one of the joys of being part of the Body of Christ.

The high point of the service, Holy Communion, is fraught with temptations for a pastor's wife, or at least *this* pastor's wife. So many people pass before me on the way to the Holy Table, so many people who have shared their lives and joys and pain with me. So many people of faith who come to the Table to be forgiven and to be strengthened in their faith. In the closeness of our special relationship, I know many of their stories and struggles, so I could be easily distracted with those details. Over the years, I've learned to turn my attention and concern for them into a prayer that Christ would bless His body and blood to them with the grace and peace only He can give. I remind myself of this special, beautiful gift and "give thanks to the Lord with my whole heart, in the company of the upright, in the congregation."

Now the service moves quickly to a close, and we praise God together for His faithfulness, for His salvation in Jesus, for the nourishment of body and blood, for allowing us to share this blessed fellowship of the saints on earth and saints above. With the Benediction, I am hurtling once again into the narthex. In my early years, a hungry, cranky little girl clung to each leg. Now, in later years, I stand in one place and talk to as many folks as I can until fatigue and Attention Exhaustion Disorder set in.

Being a pastor's wife in church on Sunday morning is an exercise in scanning the horizon for opportunities to serve and love the Body of Christ and trying to focus on my own need to worship and grow in faith. It's a balancing act, a slippery slope, and a blessed privilege—a privilege I embrace with all my heart.

Prayer: Praise be to You, Lord God, for the gift of worship and, most of all, for the gift of Christ Jesus, who is present in Word and in Sacrament, and for the forgiveness that comes through Him. Teach me to share the love and peace that come only from You each and every time there's an opportunity. In Jesus' name I pray. *Amen.*

Ruth

183

monday

Personal Study Questions:
Psalm 111:1

1. How does the worship experience described in today's faith narrative resemble your own? How does it differ?

2. How do you understand the term "praise" in the first part of verse 1? How does it differ from the "thanks" mentioned in that same verse? When might this distinction matter? when would it not?

3. The psalmist uses God's personal name throughout this psalm. The name, "*the LORD,*" is often translated "Yahweh" or "Jehovah." God revealed it to Moses at the burning bush. For that reason, it reminds the reader of the Lord's covenant-making, covenant-keeping character. (See Exodus 3:13–17.) What other names for God lead your heart into praise?

4. How does praising God "in the company of the upright" (v. 1) differ from praising God personally and individually? Why are both important for our spiritual health?

Psalm 111:2–3

Great are the works of the LORD, studied by all who delight in them. Full of splendor and majesty is His work, and His righteousness endures forever.

Thanks, Mom!

I'm curious about *everything*. It's a gift from my mom.

When I was growing up, my mom would comment, "Isn't it interesting that buttermilk lends such tenderness to pancakes?" Or, "Wouldn't you like to know more about pigs? Meat from each part of a pig tastes unique. Now, how can that be?" Or, "Today I learned that a socialite invented the dishwasher because her servants were breaking too many of her expensive dishes. Now isn't that something?" I can only imagine my sainted mom sitting for hours in front of a computer, discovering all kinds of delicious information!

Both my brothers and I are insatiably curious. I make tortuous trips through the daily newspapers, hating to miss a single article or item. I have files of clipped and saved articles, comments, and quotations that are just too clever or insightful to let pass into oblivion. I never mind waiting hours at an airport because there are people to watch and conversations to overhear and a wealth of interactions to observe. Although I am a social worker and counselor, I subscribe to *The Wall Street Journal* because its treasure trove of management information, business insight, and broad observations on contemporary culture and trends are just so *interesting.* Google.com and Ask.com make my heart beat faster.

More amazing than the miracle of hands that move and fingers that can write is the wonder of a God who is Himself perfectly righteous, hating sin and unrighteousness— the wonder of that same God loving you and me so much that He gives to us the righteousness of His dear Son, Jesus.

As the medical world discovers more about our bodies, maps genes, and reports, for example, that half a human liver can regenerate itself into a full-size organ within a few months, scientists are only now discovering what God has known all along. Adventurers and explorers simply uncover systems and miracles and principles of creation that God put into place before time began. There is nothing that exists today that is not the product of God's creative and inventive activity.

On any particular day, whether my interests are broad and inclusive or more narrowly focused, I am aware of the opportunity for "God sightings" in everything I discover and learn. Much of what *I* do is forgettable, but the psalmist observes that the works of the Lord "are studied by all who delight in them" (v. 2). As I pay attention to the world around me, I see God at work and notice the Creator's genius. It's an opportunity to pause and ponder—and be delighted.

A few years ago, I was writing a series of scripts for a video study series. In one group of scripts, I used the visual of human hands. As I learned more about hands, I would sometimes have to stop writing and just praise God for the miracle of the human hand. For example, did you know that the fingers on a human hand have no muscles? I didn't either! So how can fingers move? Fingers are controlled by tendons that transfer force and energy from the muscles in the forearm and palm to the fingers. In God's

Ruth

wonderful economy, fingers are slimmer and have more dexterity because they don't have muscles. Typing, playing the piano, and handwriting are all miracles, worked into the human design by an infinitely creative and resourceful God. As I wrote, I was discovering what God had built into the human body at its initial design, and I couldn't take in the information in a superficial or transient way and blithely move on. As *Webster's Dictionary* describes the act of pondering, I needed "to consider deeply and thoroughly" what I was learning about God as the Creator of my hands.

"Studying the great works of the Lord" leads directly to praising God! And the direct result of pausing, studying, and praising God are words of delight: "Full of splendor and majesty is His work" (v. 3). God's works are great like Himself; there is nothing in them that is mean or small or trifling. Each work is the product of infinite wisdom and power.

I am the grandmother of three little girls, five, seven, and nine years old. While much is written about the natural wonder of a child's perspective, I don't find that wonder is necessarily a first response for a child. I personally find it more of a challenge to help the girls avoid taking the natural world and the miracle of their bodies for granted. They think trees are trees; I know that trees are *amazing* in their design and effectiveness. The girls love sports and movement; I know it is a *miracle* that the human body moves with such grace and efficiency in concert with the mind. From time to time, it is my privilege to point out small wonders to them and comment, "Didn't God do a good thing?" or "Wasn't God smart to think of that?" or "God says we are 'fearfully and wonderfully made'" (Psalm 139:14). As my granddaughters grow older, my privilege will be to help them develop the daily habit of prayerfully pausing, quietly pondering, and then praising God without reservation!

Even as appreciation of God's great and mighty works opens God's world to our eyes and hearts, we chiefly praise God because "His righteousness endures forever" (Psalm 111:3). Being righteous is a part of God's character; it means He is good, honest,

Ruth

187

fair, and morally right in all He does. I assure you that as a wife, mother and grandmother, I try to be perfectly good, honest, fair, and morally right in all I do. I was raised to "make nice" and to help everyone be happy. But trying, even trying *hard,* doesn't make it happen because I still sin against God and against the people in my life. I daily need the saving love of God and the forgiveness of others.

In order to love and save us, God had to strip His Son of righteousness and lay on Him the punishment we deserve. Being righteous, just and fair, God had to punish sin; being full of mercy and undeserved love for you and me, God covers you and me in Christ's righteousness. More amazing than the miracle of hands that move and fingers that can write is the wonder of a God who is Himself perfectly righteous, hating sin and unrighteousness— the wonder of that same God loving you and me so much that He gives us the righteousness of His dear Son, Jesus. "The righteousness of God [comes] through faith in Jesus Christ for all who believe. . . . For all have sinned and fall short of the glory of God, and are justified by His grace as a gift, through the redemption that is in Christ Jesus" (Romans 3:22–24).

God's created world is worthy of awe and wonder and prayers of praise; but God's gift of salvation in Jesus invites us to new heights of praise and thanksgiving: "Amen! Blessing and glory and wisdom and thanksgiving and honor and power and might be to our God forever and ever! Amen" (Revelation 7:12).

Prayer: Creator God, I praise You for Your wondrous and awesome world, for Your incredible design of human life, for Your faithfulness to me. Savior Jesus, I praise You for the righteousness You give me so freely. Holy Spirit, I praise You for the gift of faith that is mine through the means of grace. For Jesus' sake. **Amen.**

Ruth

tuesday

Personal Study Questions:
Psalm 111:2–3

1. What details from today's faith narrative led you to ponder the Lord's goodness in the creation? in Christ Jesus?

2. Ancient Israel probably sang this psalm as the nation celebrated the Passover.

   a. As they sang about Yahweh's "great works" and "majestic works," what events do you suppose they had in mind? As you think about these works, what events come to your own mind?

   b. Which works of God would you like to study further and know more about (v. 2)?

3. The Lord is "gracious and compassionate" (v. 4) to us in our Savior, Jesus.

   a. When have you personally experienced the Lord's grace in a special way? His compassion?

   b. How would your life be different if your Lord were not gracious and compassionate?

Ruth

Psalm 111:4–8

He has caused His wondrous works to be remembered; the LORD is gracious and merciful. He provides food for those who fear Him; He remembers His covenant forever.

Where's That Brake When I Need It?

It was good to wake up yesterday morning. Well, of course, it's a gift to wake up *every* morning. But yesterday's awakening saved me from a troubling dream.

In the dream, I was driving a car, but the only direction it would go was reverse. I used the rearview mirror and the side mirrors and kept turning around in the seat as I worked to miss various objects, garage walls, and people. Raising the level of difficulty was the fact that my lap and the area around my feet were filled with "stuff," so much stuff I couldn't raise my foot to the brake, and every time

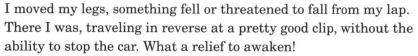

I moved my legs, something fell or threatened to fall from my lap. There I was, traveling in reverse at a pretty good clip, without the ability to stop the car. What a relief to awaken!

I didn't puzzle long over what my dream meant; it was an instant "A-ha!" moment. My life today is like driving the hard way in a direction I don't want to go—and I can't get my foot on the brake!

Within a period of about two hours before bedtime the night before, I had received three phone calls: a call from a radiologist saying my last mammogram didn't look "quite right" and he wanted to do another test and a sonogram; a call from a nurse at the home where my mom, who has Alzheimer's, is living, saying they'd found a mass on her chest wall that is likely a recurrence of the breast cancer that necessitated two mastectomies in her younger years; and a call from my husband's oncologist saying he would order a CT scan to determine whether my husband's cancer has invaded his liver. So where's that brake when I need it?

One of the advantages of growing older is that at sixty-two, I am never at a loss when I try to remember the wonders of the Lord. The more years I live, the more wonders I have to recount. And for the people of the Old Testament, *remember* meant not just "to recall mentally," but actually "to call into the present moment" that which is to be remembered. Whenever my life seems to be moving swiftly and inexorably in what I consider the wrong direction, the Holy Spirit offers to bring into the present moment, into my remembrance, the goodness of God from the past. I have embraced this practice as a spiritual discipline, a practice that exercises and strengthens my faith.

So after the barrage of distressing phone calls, I sat quietly and remembered the loving and compassionate God who shepherded me through a disrupted childhood, repeatedly provides effective medical treatment for my husband, blesses my life with caring family and friends, and who is always as good as His word when He promises to provide "food," the basic necessities of life. I have everything I need.

The discipline of remembering and allowing the blessed

Ruth

191

events from the past into my present circumstance also parallels what social scientists and counselors are learning about how we generate emotions. Emotions don't just fall out of the sky into our minds and hearts. Emotions are generated from the thoughts we think. As we assign meaning to the events and happenings in our lives, and as we evaluate the importance of those events and whether they are "good" events or "bad" events, our feelings follow our thinking and our self-talk about what is happening.

God knows I am afraid. God knows I crave control. God knows that remembering His wonders doesn't occur naturally to me. And so, in His gracious compassion, God sends His Holy Spirit to bring into the present moment His past faithfulness and to bring before the Father with sighs and groans my deepest needs.

So, for example, if I assume that my husband's liver scan will definitely reveal cancer, I will generate feelings of panic and grief and perhaps depression—even before the test takes place! However, if I call into the present and remember the faithfulness of God in the last four and a half years since my husband was diagnosed with Stage 4 cancer, I will generate emotions that reflect calmness, trust, and a certain amount of amazement at the goodness God has shown us. Remembrance is a gift that transforms my thinking and redirects my thoughts from panic to peace, from fear to trust.

"Remember my affliction. . . . My soul . . . is bowed down within me. But this I call to mind, and therefore I have hope: The steadfast love of the LORD never ceases; His mercies never come to an end" (Lamentations 3:19–22).

Cancer, Alzheimer's, and death were not part of God's original plan. God planned that we would live in fullness and health and in communion with Him forever. Adam and Eve changed that when they thought they would determine for themselves what was good and bad and follow their own inclinations rather than obey God. They were banished from the Garden of Eden so they would not eat of the Tree of Life and have to live in their sinful state forever. God promised Adam and Eve a Savior; already at the Fall, God was the very embodiment of grace and compassion (Genesis 3)!

Ruth

Adam and Eve were looking for control—no driving in reverse without a brake for them! I can identify. My gut reaction when receiving three worrisome phone calls in a row is to try to figure it out, determine which is the good and which is the bad, and then look for a way to control and direct my life, choose the good, and eliminate the bad. I want to find a way to make life go forward into a bright and guaranteed future, find a way to reach the brake and bring everything under control—*my* control. My dream of the out of control ride in reverse gear surely shows the deepest longing of my heart and reveals the challenge of trusting God in rough times.

Verse 5 of Psalm 111 calls me to a new reality, a reality foreign to my gut reaction: God knows I am afraid. God knows I crave control. God knows that remembering His wonders doesn't occur naturally to me. And so, in His gracious compassion, God sends His Holy Spirit to bring into the present moment His past faithfulness and to bring before the Father with sighs and groans my deepest needs. "Likewise the Spirit helps us in our weakness. For we do not know what to pray for as we ought, but the Spirit Himself intercedes for us with groanings too deep for words" (Romans 8:26).

And, finally, God in His compassionate graciousness has provided a Savior who makes eternity my home and therefore makes it safe to live and navigate through this life until that eternal home becomes my dwelling place. "If God is for us, who can be against us? He who did not spare His own Son but gave Him up for us all, how will He not also with Him graciously give us all things?" (Romans 8:31b–32). Since God has the big things covered, covered in the blood of the Son, I will trust God to manage everything that vexes and scares me in everyday life.

So where's that brake when I need it? The God who is gracious and compassionate, the God who has performed great wonders in the past and brings that remembrance into the present with wonderment and awe, the God who has promised to provide everything I need and has covenanted to be my God forever—God Himself holds the brake. He will bring the distressing, confusing

Ruth

and breakneck ride to a halt when the time is right and when it is best for me. The brake is safely in His hands and "underneath [me] are the everlasting arms" (Deuteronomy 33:27b).

Prayer: Gracious God, whatever happens in my life today, remind me that You are in control, You are in the driver's seat. Keep me always in Your everlasting arms, in the palm of Your hand. I ask this in the name of Your Son, Jesus Christ, who lives and reigns with You, now and forever. Amen.

Ruth

Personal Study Questions:
Psalm 111:4–8

1. In verses 4–5, the psalmist encourages us to call to mind the gamut of blessings God has given, everything from the salad we ate at lunch yesterday to the gift of eternal life itself—life with God, both now and forever.

   a. Recall—"call into the present moment"—God's goodness to you in the past, as today's faith narrative suggests. How might this discipline of recollection, repeated regularly, strengthen your faith?

   b. What do all these blessings reveal about our Lord's involvement in the lives of His children?

2. Human beings often break their promises. How sure are the Lord's covenant promises (vv. 6–8)? What does that say about your security today and forever—no matter what news you might receive or what experiences you might encounter?

Ruth

Psalm 111:6–9

He has shown His people the power of His works, in giving them the inheritance of the nations. The works of His hands are faithful and just; all His precepts are trustworthy; they are established forever and ever, to be performed with faithfulness and uprightness. He sent redemption to His people; He has commanded His covenant forever. Holy and awesome is His name!

Staying Put

All my life I've been looking for things that would *stay put*.

I like the fact that my marriage is for life. I like friends who stay friends for a lifetime. I like the way God has given me brothers who can't become un-brothers.

I think it is good to have principles and values that are learned and embraced in early life and remain valued throughout life. I think it's a good thing to take the furniture off the moving van, put it in its place, and leave it there for as long as we live in the

house. I've had the same hairstyle for decades, and I replace clothes only when they become threadbare or indecently out of style.

My desire for stability extends to other people's behavior too. I don't like it when people change. About twenty years ago, my husband and I were having a now-famous argument when he voiced an opinion different from one he had held, say, fifteen years before that. I raised my voice and said in indignation, "Well, you've never thought *that* before!" As soon as the words were out of my mouth, they rolled back to my own ears and I said to myself, *So, he doesn't get to think any new thoughts, huh?*

The most common cause of stress is reality. For me, that reality is embodied in things that change, shift, and move—in short, the ambiguities of life. I feel best when life is tidy and neat and predictable and my ducks are all in a row, and, of course, when all the forces of life converge for the express purpose of making me feel safe and secure. I once read a definition of *maturity*: being able to tolerate the ambiguities of life. Ouch.

Looking for lifelong stability in the midst of an unstable world is like going to a hardware store to buy milk. No matter how many times you walk up and down the aisles of the hardware store, you still won't find milk. I now know that the kind of security and stability I've wanted all my life is found in a living relationship with God.

When I was six or seven years old, I was awake in my bed one night, waiting for sleep. I think I was praying my nightly prayers. God chose that very moment to assure me, in a way that I believed immediately, that He would never leave me or forsake me, that His love was the ground on which I would always stand. "I will never leave you nor forsake you" (Hebrews 13:5b). The Holy Spirit caused me to believe those words, and they have always proved the counterpoint, the tension, the faith challenge to my lifelong quest for a life that *stays put.*

When I read Psalm 111:6–9, I can almost see poet David's hair on fire with the certainty of God's power, faithfulness, and steadfastness! He makes the point in several different ways, just

Ruth

so the reader doesn't miss it: God is powerful enough to give the people He loves the lands of other nations (v. 6)! Everything God does is stable, trustworthy, and cannot be undone (v. 7a)! The rules (precepts) He's given us to live by are for our good and to bring Him glory; not a word of those divine commands can be changed or thwarted. God's rules are like an owner's manual for a healthy and holy life (vv. 7b–8)!

Looking for lifelong stability in the midst of an unstable world is like going to a hardware store to buy milk. No matter how many times you walk up and down the aisles of the hardware store, you still won't find milk.

And here are more smoking-hot assurances from God through David: everything God does is honest and true and cannot be destroyed (v. 8). God is the very standard of Honest and True and Enduring. Talk about stability! Talk about things that do not change! What really matters is not going to change: God's powerful provision for His people, God's trustworthy and stable nature, God's directions for living on earth. These things will not change, and so I have a firm place to stand as I deal with the instability and change I so hate in everyday life.

In light of God's stability and His provision of a firm place to stand in His presence, my feeble efforts to keep things the same seem pathetic and untrusting. When I lose sight of the sweeping, heaven-and-earth-filling Source of all things, I look around in panic for my own solutions to the problem. My own solutions are seldom good, never adequate, certainly not lasting.

But, wait! There's more! David speaks to my deepest need, my need for a Savior: "He sent redemption to His people; He has commanded His covenant forever. Holy and awesome is His name!" (v. 9). Not only am I invited to stand in the stable, sure place of a faithful, steadfast, and trustworthy God; now I can stand forgiven with the righteous because God has given us Jesus.

In David's time, God time and again saved the Israelites from calamity: He rescued them from the Egyptians (Exodus 14), provided manna in the desert (Exodus 16), and repeatedly saved them from predator nations. In Psalm 111:9, David is saying, "See, God

Ruth

is faithful. He never stops loving and saving you." In my lifetime, I see Jesus as the guarantee that God is faithful to His promise to send a Savior and that He never stops loving or saving me.

God promised a Savior to Adam and Eve and, thus, to all His people. When His people looked elsewhere for a savior, God made a new covenant, this time calling for the blood of His Son, Jesus (see Hebrews 8:8–13). "How much more will the blood of Christ, who through the eternal Spirit offered Himself without blemish to God, purify our conscience from dead works to serve the living God!" (Hebrews 9:14).

I believe that the God who does not, *cannot* change has made a promise that gives me a safe place to stand for all eternity. By the Holy Spirit's power, I can set aside the drive and need to make my own life and times stable, to make everything *stay put*. In his second letter to the Corinthian Christians, St. Paul talks about the stability, the dependability of the message of Christ that he is delivering: "As surely as God is faithful, our word to you has not been Yes and No. For the Son of God, Jesus Christ, whom we proclaimed among you, Silvanus and Timothy and I, was not Yes and No, but in Him it is always Yes. For all the promises of God find their Yes in Him. . . . And it is God who establishes us and you in Christ" (2 Corinthians 1:18–20a, 21).

Established in Christ. Now *that's* the stable and secure place I want to be. And by God's grace, that's where I stand. Yes!

Prayer: Dear God, You never change! When the realities of this world cause me to feel unstable and afraid, help me to know that You are faithful, trustworthy, and eternal. I praise You and thank You that I can stand firm and secure in Your grace, through the work of Your Son. In His name I pray. Amen.

Ruth

thursday

1. This passage no doubt reminded ancient Israel of the Lord's deliverance of the nation from slavery in Egypt (Exodus 12:1–13, 40–42). How does Psalm 111:9 fit that event?

2. As we read verse 9 through New Testament eyes today, it reminds us also of Good Friday and Easter Sunday (1 Corinthians 5:7–8). How so?

3. How do *both* events evoke the words "Holy and awesome is His name" (v. 9) from the lips of God's people?

4. How do *both* events create unshakable faith in your unchangeable God whose grace toward you "stays put"?

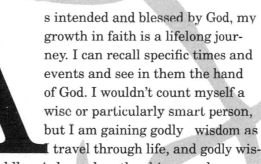

Psalm 111:10

The fear of the LORD is the beginning of wisdom; all those who practice it have a good understanding. His praise endures forever!

The Good Life

As intended and blessed by God, my growth in faith is a lifelong journey. I can recall specific times and events and see in them the hand of God. I wouldn't count myself a wise or particularly smart person, but I am gaining godly wisdom as I travel through life, and godly wisdom trumps worldly wisdom when the chips are down.

"The fear of the LORD" encompasses many aspects of my relationship with God. The fear of the Lord embraces the intimacy of quiet and prayer and the awe of a God who would send a Savior to earth if I were the only sinner in need. The fear of the Lord is the Holy Spirit growing my love for and commitment to God's commands and the will to obey Him. The fear of the Lord is the still, small voice of the Spirit who nudges and helps and gives me insight when I can't imagine what to say or how to think about something that has happened.

We moved to Denver the first time in 1983, and it was a whirlwind life. My husband jumped right into his work as senior pastor at a large urban congregation, our two daughters were in late grade school and early high school, and I had a house to whip into shape. Add the usual: driving kids to school activities, keeping a home, laundry, meals, and involvement in church activities. It took about eighteen months, but the inevitable collision of over-activity and frail flesh finally happened: I was worn out, inside and out.

The good life begins with the realization that God is God and I don't have to be.

So, as one of my therapeutic endeavors (we social workers have a language for this!), I determined that I would watch the sun set behind the mountains. We certainly didn't have a panoramic view of the mountains, but I could see the sunset in the small sliver of light between two trees. Sounded like a plan!

The first evening I was prepared for a great experience. I had sent out the word that this was my quiet time and woe to anyone who interrupted me! Five minutes of lovely sunset. Then ten minutes. I'm getting antsy. Gripping the arms of the chair. Thirteen minutes. Eighteen. I'm watching my watch. *How long does it take the sun to set anyway?*

I obviously needed a new approach, a new motivation, a clean heart. It wasn't the beauty of the sunset that was going to give me the breathing space I needed and the inner renewal; God's Spirit was telling me that the quiet and peace I craved would be waiting for me in the Scriptures and in quiet prayer, in awe and reverence for the Lord.

So I tried a new tack and a new location and a new focus: quiet time in the Word, quiet prayer, learning to know and fear the Lord as He revealed Himself in Word and Spirit. Yet the inevitable excuses surfaced: today's too busy, no time for prayer, no time to be in the Word, no time to sit and listen to the Lord. The fear of the Lord, intimacy with the Lord, open and loving com-

Ruth

munication with the Lord create an internal struggle with all that makes me truly miserable. The good life began with the beginning of wisdom and my realization that I had to view blessed time with the Lord as a discipline, a choice, a holy obligation that would mature my faith and enrich and calm my daily life.

The good life begins in the fear of God. Growing in love and awe and reverence for God produces a cascading stream of wisdom and maturity, in faith, in personality, and in relationships. Although I am a trained social worker, I am often at a loss for words in the presence of a grieving friend, a distraught neighbor, a young person without direction, a co-worker who is searching for life's purpose. How can that be since it's not the right words but a right *heart* that truly serves another? So I pray on the spot for words that will point to Christ, I ask God to remove my preoccupation with my own discomfort, I beseech God for the compassion and wisdom only He can supply. So in awe of God's help, so full of trust that He will not leave me without His very own compassionate heart, so dependent on God to give me words, His words, I beg for God, with whom wisdom begins.

It's my favorite bumper sticker: "Don't believe everything you think." Just as emotions are flighty, here today and gone tomorrow, and just as moods come and go, thoughts reflect personal history, sometimes faulty conclusions, and self-deception. Don't believe everything you think; just because you think it doesn't make it true. Those statements are good reminders that I need to submit even my thoughts to the lordship of Christ. "We destroy arguments and every lofty opinion raised against the knowledge of God, and take every thought captive to obey Christ" (2 Corinthians 10:5). Challenging my thoughts is a concept foreign to the unbelieving world; challenging my thoughts is part of how I understand the fear of the Lord, the first place God deserves in my mind as well as my heart. I know that only when every thought is obedient to Christ will I be truly wise.

For Lent one year, I gave up being defensive. I deliberately became aware of all the times I thought I had to protect my reputation or manage another person's impression of just how good

Ruth

and wonderful I am. It would have been a *lot* easier to give up chocolate! At every turn, I caught myself trying to set the record straight: I didn't say that, I didn't mean that, I intended a good thing, I didn't sin, I didn't wish someone ill, I didn't act bossy and know-it-all. It was exhausting, this defending myself against the truth of my sinful nature. I am redeemed by Christ, but still my sinful nature rises! St. Paul and I got to be pals: "For I delight in the law of God, but I see in my members another law waging war against the law of my mind and making me captive to the law of sin that dwells in my members" (Romans 7:22–23).

The fear of the Lord is the awe I have for the God who sent His Son, Jesus, to redeem a miserable, muddling sinner who tries to do it all and be it all and make all of life follow her own self-serving rules. The good life begins with the realization that God is God and I don't have to be, that I must bear the earthly consequences for my sin, but Christ has borne the eternal consequences for my sin. The good life begins when I can say with St. Paul, "Wretched man that I am! Who will deliver me from this body of death? Thanks be to God through Jesus Christ our Lord!" (Romans 7:24–25a).

The good life has begun . . . thanks to God!

Prayer: Dear Redeemer, Jesus Christ, my heart is full with gratitude and awe for all You have done for me and for the good life I have through Your mercy and forgiveness. Send Your Holy Spirit to sustain my faith in You and to grow in godly wisdom. In Your name. **Amen.**

Ruth

Personal Study Questions:
Psalm 111:10

1. What is the "fear of the LORD" mentioned in verse 10?

2. In what way does it form the foundation for true wisdom?

3. How do we "practice" this fear?

4. How does it lead to the good life in ways absolutely nothing else can?

Group Bible Study for Week 6
Psalm 111

1. Which faith narrative(s) from this week brought special insight and comfort to your heart? Explain.

2. Praise acts as a set of bookends for this psalm (vv. 1, 10). What makes that appropriate?

3. Compare Psalm 73:1 with 111:1.

   a. How are the "pure in heart" from 73:1 and the "whole heart" of 111:1 alike?

   b. From where do God's people get a heart like that? (See Psalm 37:4.)

   c. How does a pure heart grow out of the "wisdom" and "understanding" commended in Psalm 111:10?

4. Review the events of the first Passover by reading Exodus 11:1–8 and 12:29–32. Then read Psalm 111 aloud. What made this psalm fitting for use in worship at Passover time in ancient Israel?

5. Review the effects of Good Friday by reading 2 Corinthians 5:14–21. Then read Psalm 111 aloud a second time. What makes this psalm fitting for use in worship as God's people commemorate our Savior's death and resurrection?

6. How might we understand—in a New Testament sense—the fact that God has shown His people His power by "giving [us] the inheritance of the nations" (Psalm 111:6)? (See also Matthew 28:18–20.)

7. This volume of *A New Song* ties together six psalms under the title "Planted by Streams of Water: Psalms of Divine Wisdom."

a. Psalms 1 and 111 have much in common. Psalms 34, 37, 73, and 49 are alike in many respects, as well. But how do all six psalms fit together under the title they were given in this volume?

b. What will you take away from this study? In other words, how have you grown in divine wisdom, how have you sunk your roots more deeply into the soil of Christ's love for you these past six weeks? (See Colossians 2:6–7.)

c. For what will you praise Jesus as you close your time together today? For what will you thank Him?

BOOK ONE

Small-Group Leader Guide

This guide will help guide you in discovering the truths of God's Word. It is not, however, exhaustive, nor is it designed to be read aloud during your session.

1. Before you begin, spend some time in prayer, asking God to strengthen your faith through a study of His Word. The Scriptures were written so that we might believe in Jesus Christ and have life in His name (John 20:31). Also, pray for participants by name.

2. Before your meeting, review the session material, read the Bible passages, and answer the questions in the spaces provided. Your familiarity with the session will give you confidence as you lead the group.

3. As a courtesy to participants, begin and end each session on time.

4. Have a Bible dictionary or similar resource handy to look up difficult or unfamiliar names, words, and places. Ask participants to help you in this task. Be sure that each participant has a Bible and a study guide.

5. Ask for volunteers to read introductory paragraphs and Bible passages. A simple "thank you" will encourage them to volunteer again.

6. See your role as a conversation facilitator rather than a lecturer. Don't be afraid to give participants time to answer questions. By name, thank each participant who answers; then invite other input. For example, you may say, "Thank you, Maggie. Would anyone else like to share?"

7. Now and then, summarize aloud what the group has learned by studying God's Word.

8. Remember that the questions provided are discussion starters. Allow participants to ask questions that relate to the session. However, keep discussions on track with the session.

9. Everyone is a learner! If you don't know the answer to a question, simply tell participants that you need time to look at more Scripture passages or to ask your pastor.

Week 1, Psalm 1

Personal Study Questions

Monday—Psalm 1:1

1. The word *blessed* indicates a positive state of being, one worthy of envy by those who have not attained it. However, as Scripture uses the word *blessed*, it does not mean "happy" in the sense of "everything's going my way." Rather, it conveys the idea of enjoying God's favor. The New Testament uses this same term to express "the distinctive joy which comes through participation in the divine kingdom."

2. Answers will vary.

3. Answers will vary.

4. Answers will vary.

Tuesday—Psalm 1:2

1. Answers will vary.

2. Answers will vary.

3. Answers will vary.

4. Answers will vary.

Wednesday—Psalm 1:3

1. Answers will vary.

2. Answers will vary.

3. Answers will vary.

Thursday—Psalm 1:4–5

1. Certainly, in eternity, the wicked endure torment beyond our imagination. However, here on earth, they also endure the meaninglessness, frustration, worry, and turmoil of life lived apart from the living God, who loves all people in Christ. Of course, many of those who live

apart from Christ would deny a need for His companionship and forgiveness. As many psalms we will study over the next six weeks will show, not all unbelievers see themselves as miserable—seeing reality as they do only through the lens of their present circumstances. Christians who witness to unbelieving friends need to examine their own presuppositions carefully ahead of time and tailor their words and deeds of witness wisely and prayerfully.

2. Like Eve, we enjoy the blessings of the incredible universe the Creator bequeathed to His human creatures. Like Eve, we, too, have sinned and need a Savior. Many other commonalities could, of course, be mentioned.

3. Jesus purchased for us a priceless robe of righteousness—right standing before God despite our sins. By living a perfectly obedient earthly life in our place and then suffering and dying the death we had, by our sins, deserved, our King earned this robe for us. Sadly, many refuse this robe. In some cases, they believe their own character, intentions, and good works should be enough to secure God's favor (for example, "I'm a good person"; "I meant well"; "I invest twenty hours a week in volunteer endeavors"). Some also believe God "grades on the curve" ("I'm far more kind and helpful to others than *that* person"). Some see the good things they do as somehow canceling out or making up for their wrongs (which they consider "small" and "insignificant"). In all these ways, they wrap the tattered, filthy robe of self-righteousness around themselves and go on rejecting the spotless robe of righteousness the Savior wants to give them as His free gift to them.

4. See 2 Corinthians 5:21.

Friday—Psalm 1:6

1. Answers will vary.
2. Answers will vary.
3. Talking and even thinking about hell and the eternal punishment that awaits the wicked can sound hopelessly intolerant, antiquated, and unfashionable. However, Scripture clearly teaches that hell exists and that those who reject Christ will spend eternity there. Time is short, and Christ is coming! Jesus once told His disciples, "We must work

the works of Him who sent Me while it is day; night is coming, when no one can work" (John 9:4). May the Holy Spirit work this sense of urgency in us!

4. Answers will vary.

Group Bible Study

1. Let participants discuss this. Psalm 1 expresses the blessedness of those who read, mark, learn, and inwardly digest not just its teachings, but also the teachings of the entire Psalter, and indeed, all of Scripture.

2. As the notes for Day 1 pointed out, the word *blessed* indicates a positive state of being. The righteous are not always "happy" as our culture would define that term. Yet "blessedness" trumps "happiness" any day for any number of reasons. Other psalms this book will examine dig more deeply into this. However, the contrasts presented in Psalm 1 between the wicked and the righteous cause us to pause and think!

3. Psalm 1 contains several contrasts: the stability of the righteous vs. the insecurity of the wicked; the fruitfulness of the righteous vs. the scoffing and sin of the wicked; the peace of the righteous in the judgment vs. the eternal death of the wicked; the companionship of the righteous in the "congregation" of the faithful vs. the rejection of the wicked from that company. Other contrasts are possible.

These contrasts both warn and comfort us. God has provided a way of escape from the fate of the wicked—faith clings to the gracious work of our Savior, Jesus, on our behalf, on His death for us and His glorious resurrection. He is our peace, both now and forever.

4. Jesus earned the blessed standing before God that Psalm 1 describes. He is the "blessed man" the psalm describes. He deserved that blessedness Himself, and He now gives it to us. He has connected us by faith to Himself. Now we, too, can bear abundant fruit. (See John 15:1–8 in this regard.)

5. Answers will vary. Share with one another as honestly as you can do so. Then base your closing prayer on your discussion.

Week 2, Psalm 34

Personal Study Questions

Monday—Psalm 34:1–7

1. Answers will vary.
2. Answers will vary.
3. Answers will vary.
4. Answers will vary.

Tuesday—Psalm 34:8–10

1. Answers will vary.
2. Answers will vary.
3. Answers will vary.

Wednesday—Psalm 34:11–14

1. David commends the "fear of the LORD," refraining from all evil speech, presumably including sins like blasphemy, gossip, coarse words, hurtful and loveless words, and the like. He also wants his students to avoid lies, to turn from all evil, to work for the good of others, and to live in peace with all.

2. Answers will vary.

3. Each of the four Gospels (Matthew, Mark, Luke, and John) includes dozens of examples. (See also 1 Peter 2: 21–23.)

4. Answers will vary.

Thursday—Psalm 34:15–18

1. Answers will vary.

2. Verses 15–16 contrast God's attitude toward the "righteous" with His attitude toward "those who do evil." By God's grace, through faith in Jesus and His cross and resurrection, we are "the righteous." (See 2 Corinthians 5:21.)

3. Answers will vary.

Friday—Psalm 34:19–22

1. Answers will vary.

2. Verse 19 acknowledges that the "afflictions of the righteous" are many. The text quickly adds, however, the promise that "the LORD delivers [us] out of them all"!

3. Jesus put up with Satan's temptations, the faithlessness of His friends, and the taunts of His enemies. He lived through storms, hunger, cold, heat, and loneliness. He endured many afflictions, yet God did deliver Him out of them all. (Compare v. 20 with John 19:36.)

4. Answers will vary.

Group Bible Study

1. Answers will vary.

2. David wrote Psalm 34 based on his own intimate familiarity with life's adversities and the Lord's faithfulness. David could pray the words of the psalm in the same way we can—by faith. God's promises are true, yes, and amen, whether or not we see evidence of that with our physical eyes at any given moment.

3. God's angels protect His children. Because the angels minister to us, we can be sure we will be safe and lack no good thing. God deals with us in His perfect wisdom. If any change in our circumstances would be better for us at any point, our God would enact that change. Therefore, as we endure hardships and challenges, we can ask God to remove them, certainly. But we can also ask for faith to see our Lord at work in our situation for our ultimate good and His eternal glory. Other connections and insights are certainly possible.

4. Let volunteers comment.

5. The "fear of the LORD" (vv. 9, 11) involves our holding Him in reverence and awe, in honor and praise. This fear instills within us a deep desire to avoid offending Him in any way or incurring guilt and His righteous judgment because of our disobedience. This contrasts sharply with

the fears brought on by unbelief and sinful self-reliance.

Those whose hearts hold godly fear are also "brokenhearted" and "crushed in spirit"; they "cry" to the Lord in time of need and "take refuge" in Him. They are "blessed." In this sense, being blessed and fearing the Lord both describe the same state.

6. Let volunteers comment.

Week 3, Psalm 37

Personal Study Questions

Monday—Psalm 37:1–11

1. Answers will vary.

2. Verses 3–4 promise that our Lord will give us "the desires of our heart." Think about times He has done this for you.

3. When the righteous still today see the wicked enjoying mountains of material blessings, we likely find our hearts filled with temptations to envy. Answers to questions (b) and (c) will vary.

Tuesday—Psalm 37:12–20

1. All the contrasts point to the long-term advantages the righteous enjoy. In the end, everything on earth will be burned up in the judgment. Only a relationship with Christ and the inheritance kept for us in heaven will endure. While the wicked may look very "wise" today, their pseudo-blessedness is shallow and temporary. Living in the fear of the Lord is the only truly wise path.

2. Answers will vary.

Wednesday—Psalm 37:21–26

1. Answers will vary.

2. Answers will vary.

Thursday—Psalm 37:27–34

1. Answers will vary, depending on each individual's circumstances and the particular strategies Satan chooses to use in her life.

2. Answers will vary.

3. Answers will vary.

Friday—Psalm 37:35–40

1. The wicked, ruthless person spreads out like a tree (Psalm 37:35–36). However, it soon dies and decays. The tree described in Psalm 1 flourishes beside the stream, righteous and relying on God's wisdom as opposed to worldly self-reliance.

2. Temporarily, those without a true relationship with Christ often do achieve the goals they set out to achieve. However, having set priorities based on their own limited insight, their ultimate failure is both predictable and very, very tragic.

3. Answers will vary. Jesus is always a refuge for repentant sinners. We cling to His cross for hope and renewed courage.

4. Answers will vary.

Group Bible Study

1. Answers will vary.

2. Answers will vary.

3. Let participants comment, citing specific verses and/or phrases from the psalm.

4. Let volunteers share, as they feel comfortable in doing so.

5. Answers will vary.

6. Answers will vary.

7. Answers will vary.

Week 4, Psalm 49

Personal Study Questions

Monday—Psalm 49:1–4

1. The psalmist invites us to hear his wisdom, promising that the meditation of his heart will produce understanding.

2. Verses 1–2 address "all people," "all inhabitants of the world," the "low and high, rich and poor together."

3. Answers will vary.

4. Answers will vary, but will likely include our sinful flesh, the forgetfulness of our hearts, our fear that God may not have our best interests at heart—in short, unbelief.

5. The forgiveness that flows from Jesus' cross and open tomb brings peace and hope for us at all times, especially times of guilt and shame. May we never take this precious gift for granted!

Tuesday—Psalm 49:5

1. The psalmist puzzles over reasons behind his fear during times of trouble. Why does it bother him so much when the wicked people around him seem to prosper and, as they cheat the godly, boast in their achievements?

2. Our sinful flesh would much rather make excuses than make confession. From childhood onward, we look for ways to justify ourselves. Sinful pride keeps us from wanting to face the truth.

3. We already know what God's answer will be when we confess our sins and ask for mercy. In Jesus, we are forgiven! This gives us the courage necessary to confess.

Wednesday—Psalm 49:6–9

1. Jesus ransomed us. (See 1 Peter 1:18–19.)

2. Psalm 49:9 promises life that never ends.

3. Knowing our Father's total acceptance of us in Jesus encourages us to rely on Him for help in every time of need.

Thursday—Psalm 49:10–15

1. Verses 10–11 explain that even the wise die—along with the "fool" and the "stupid."

2. In essence, death destroys the opportunity for a meaningful life—if, that is, the cemetery is the end of the line for us. Human accomplishments quickly fade from the awareness of the living. (If you doubt that, ask yourself who won last year's Super Bowl or who is this year's poet laureate or who was president of the United States before Ronald Reagan!) "Out of sight, out of mind"—it's very true!

3. Death "shepherds" the wicked; Jesus shepherds us! What a difference a relationship with our Savior makes! Psalm 49:15 points us toward the ransom that made that relationship possible.

4. Verses 12–15 help answer the writer's original riddle by contrasting the eternal life that belongs to the righteous and the temporary prosperity that brings happiness into the lives of the wicked. His words show that he sees the foolishness of fearing those who temporarily make his life miserable (vv. 5–6). True wisdom looks at circumstances through the lens of eternity.

Friday—Psalm 49:16–20

1. Answers will vary. Verse 17 arguably comes closest to expressing the same idea.

2. Answers will vary, but they will focus on the blessings a true faith relationship with Jesus brings into our lives.

3. Several answers, all drawn from the faith narrative, are possible.

Group Bible Study

1. Both psalms were written with the intent to teach. Both point

the reader to the truly wise outlook on life one gains by being "planted by streams of water" (Psalm 1:3).

2. Everyone needs the wisdom the psalmist offers; it is not common sense. The finest university education cannot create it in us. Only God gives this wisdom, and we must come to Him for it or live (and die!) without it.

Let several individuals in the group share the paraphrases of verses 5–6 that they develop.

People today often ask the question the psalmist asks, commonly in times of difficulty or when it seems life has treated them unfairly.

3. Work together to detail the ways the psalmist describes the lot of the ungodly, both here on earth and in eternity. Answers to question (c) will vary.

4. Several verses in the psalm describe the future we, in our sins, deserve, among them verses 12, 14, 17, and 20. Verses 7–9 and 15 point forward to the ransom Christ paid on the cross to win us back to Himself. See Tuesday's faith narrative for a discussion of our Lord's incarnation and its importance.

5. Answers will vary.

6. Answers will vary.

Week 5, Psalm 73

Personal Study Questions

Monday—Psalm 73:1–3

1. The scribes and Pharisees of Jesus' day focused on keeping the letter of their mostly man-made laws and on seeing to it that others conformed to these laws. Jesus focused on being in a right relationship with God, one available only by His grace through faith. The Law always condemns; the Gospel always blesses. As religious "leaders," the scribes and Pharisees should have *known* and *shown* this. Instead, they rejected God's will for themselves and their followers. This sorry state drew

Jesus' "Woe!"

2. When one focuses one's heart fully on God and on the great blessing of belonging to Him, no room remains for envy and other sinful attitudes. This fact is, of course, Law and condemns all of us, for none are perfectly pure in heart. Only in Jesus' heart of pardon and love do we find peace.

3. Answers will vary.

Tuesday—Psalm 73:4–12

1. Answers will vary.

2. Answers will vary.

3. See Romans 2:4. God's kindness is intended to lead us to repentance. Instead, it leads the wicked into misusing God's gifts and an even more profound self-focus.

4. Answers will vary. Note that life's troubles and challenges are not, in and of themselves, a means of grace. We've all known people whose troubles made them bitter, not better. Rather, in times of trouble and challenge, God wants to draw us closer to Himself through the true means of grace—His Word and the Sacraments.

5. Things aren't always what they seem. Situations that may seem bad can, under the blessing of God, turn out for our ultimate good. It's not wise to evaluate external events using only our own flawed judgment.

Wednesday—Psalm 73:13–17

1. The contrasts are striking, especially as the psalmist considers them in a long-range—that is to say, eternal—context.

2. Answers will vary.

3. In kindness (Romans 2:4), God leads us to repentance for our eternal good.

4. The psalmist retreats to "the sanctuary of God." So can we. In repentant faith, we always find there a Father's welcome, complete forgiveness, and the courage to resume our various daily callings. From the sanctuary, we see our lives and opportunities through the lens of divine wisdom.

Thursday—Psalm 73:18–24

1. Asaph confesses bitterness and the kind of brutish ignorance to which we all revert when we fail to look at circumstances in the light of divine wisdom. He has "lost his grip on reality" because he has forgotten whose he is and whom he serves. (See Acts 27:23.) In a similar way, we sometimes forget our baptismal identity and fall into bitterness, perhaps even envying those who don't know Christ!

2. Verse 23 begins with what some scholars have called "God's great nevertheless"! Yes, we "daily sin much and indeed deserve nothing but punishment." But God is rich in mercy and sent Jesus to die for us. Our Lord holds our right hand (v. 23) as tenderly as a Father does and will "receive [us] to glory" (v. 24) when our lives here on earth end. Here is one of the Gospel's greatest mysteries and evidence that our Savior-God's wisdom lies far beyond human understanding!

We *are* righteous in heaven's eyes, right now. Our sins, in essence, have nothing to do with it! As time will allow, consider Genesis 20:1–17 in this context. Here, Abraham fails miserably to trust the Lord. He lies and places his wife, Sarah, in terrible jeopardy. He gives Abimelech a pitiful excuse for his sins, ruining a prime opportunity to witness regarding the goodness of the Lord. Yet, note verse 7—the Lord seemingly ignores all the fault in Abraham, even honoring him in Abimelech's dream and treating Abraham as the hero of the story. Human wisdom does not comprehend such mercy, but God surrounds us with His favor, even as He did Abraham, and all on account of Jesus, the Messiah, and the covenant relationship He has established with us—for Abraham in circumcision and for us in our Baptism.

3. Answers will vary.

Friday—Psalm 73:23–28

1. God grants us His protection, presence, counsel, strength, life with Him eternally when our lives here on earth end, and even more besides. Think about your own experience with each blessing the psalmist mentions.

2. Think of specific instances in your own life. Answers will vary.

3. The last two verses (vv. 27–28) sum up the contrasts described

throughout the rest of the psalm, closing this wisdom psalm on a note of triumph.

Group Bible Study

1. Encourage volunteers to share. Answers will vary.

2. Answers will vary. Consider having individuals in your group pair up to work on this; then share results with the whole group. Don't let this become merely a mechanical task—many insights about content and meaning can grow out of engaging the text in this way.

3. Let participants share their insights as your group considers all three of these wisdom psalms.

4. When we lose sight of our identity as the baptized children of God, we begin to adopt the pseudo-wisdom of the world system around us. That wisdom causes us to act in ways contrary to the will and true wisdom of our Father in heaven. (Compare St. Paul's comments in 1 Corinthians 3:2–4.)

5. Both Psalm 73:15 and 28 focus on the believer's witness—during times of temptation, envy, and stress (v. 15) and in times of faith (v. 28). Again, the contrast is marked.

6. This series of questions contrasts worldly wisdom (focused primarily on material prosperity and amassing wealth, attaining the good life, here on earth) with the divine wisdom (focused on an eternal relationship with God in Christ). Answers will vary, depending on the insights of the group.

7. The question calls for an opinion and will create opportunities for participants to encourage one another in the unshakable promises of God.

Week 6, Psalm 111

Personal Study Questions

Monday—Psalm 111:1

1. Answers will vary. Think not only in terms of format, but also in terms of what happens to your heart in God's presence.

2. In general, praise focuses on the Lord's attributes—on who He is as our powerful, all-wise, merciful, gracious, eternal, glorious Savior-God. Thanksgiving, on the other hand, focuses on what God has done, especially what He has done for us. Hymns and prayers often intertwine the two, combining both praise and thanks in the same hymn or prayer. Usually this matters very little, but if we consistently exclude one or the other, we miss out on some of the encouragement and hope God wants us to have as we consider His goodness.

3. Answers will vary.

4. Both personal devotional time and times of corporate worship are important to our spiritual health and well-being. Scripture commends both (e.g., Psalm 111:1; Hebrews 10:25; Psalm 42:8; Luke 6:12).

Tuesday—Psalm 111:2–3

1. Answers will vary.

2. See Exodus 1:1–14:30 for events ancient Israel probably recalled as they sang this psalm, praising God for His "great works" and "wondrous works." As we read them, we likely think of Calvary's cross and Jesus' open tomb.

3. Answers will vary.

Wednesday—Psalm 111:4–8

1. Answers will vary.

2. The Lord's covenant promises (vv. 6–8) are "faithful," "just," and absolutely "trustworthy" forever and ever. This creates confidence in our

hearts, no matter what happens.

Thursday—Psalm 111:6–9

1. Psalm 111:9 recalls the "redemption" in the Exodus, God rescuing His "firstborn"—the people of Israel, descendents of Abraham and heirs to the covenant promises Yahweh gave to Abraham.

2. The verse also calls to our minds the redemption Jesus won for us on Calvary's cross, bearing our sins, dying our death, and making us God's righteous children forever.

3. What a wonderful, saving God we serve! Answers will vary.

4. Answers will vary. Refer to today's faith narrative.

Friday—Psalm 111:10

1. The "fear of the LORD" (v. 10) is the only truly wise response to His majesty, holiness, and mercy toward us in Jesus. It includes awe, reverence, honor, and an altogether fitting, proper ambition to avoid attitudes or actions that would offend Him.

2. Western culture has for decades tried to create a picture of God as simply a somewhat "more advanced" human being. In that vein, someone quipped, "God made man in His own image, and now man has returned the favor." Only when we recognize our own creatureliness and in humility admit what we by our sins and rebellion have deserved do we see the need for a Savior and begin to treasure the gifts Jesus offers us freely in love. As the psalmist wrote, "The fear of the LORD is the beginning of wisdom" (Psalm 111:10; see also Psalm 50:19–22).

3. We "practice" this "fear" by fully relying on the Holy Spirit to create repentance and faith in our hearts and then living out of our baptismal identity as God's dearly loved, adopted daughters.

4. This lifestyle is anchored in reality, in true, divine wisdom. Much of the time, it leads us to act in ways that the world's citizens consider downright foolish. But on Judgment Day, the wisdom of living lives of repentant faith will become obvious. (See 1 Corinthians 3:13.)

Group Bible Study

1. Answers will vary.

2. The wisdom of God and His wonderful promises fill the psalm with hope. This makes praise appropriate as an introduction and conclusion.

3. The "pure in heart" of Psalm 73 and the "whole heart" of Psalm 111 describe the same phenomenon—a life focused on a single priority, a life wholly dedicated to God in Christ. We cannot work up this kind of focus by trying hard or following some effort-based formula. Rather, God creates it in us as we continue to place ourselves under the means of grace—hearing the Word and receiving the Sacraments. The desire for this kind of single focus exists only in hearts made wise by the Spirit's work within us. (See Psalm 51:10.)

4. Let volunteers comment. Psalm 111:9 recalls the "redemption" in the Exodus, God rescuing "His people"—the people of Israel, descendants of Abraham and heirs to the covenant promises Yahweh gave to Abraham.

5. Let volunteers comment. Psalm 111:9 also calls to mind the redemption Jesus won for us on Calvary's cross, bearing our sins, dying our death, and making us God's righteous children forever.

6. The explosive growth of the Christian faith in the first century and its continuing growth worldwide today testify to the Holy Spirit's power to conquer the nations through the love of Jesus. (See Psalm 2 and Jesus' parables in Matthew 13:31–33.) We get to take part in that expansion as we share the Gospel message with those around us, and as we help to send and support workers who make kingdom growth their life's work.

7. Let volunteers comment. Answers will vary.